P9-DCX-241

PATRICK & BEATRICE HAGGERTY LIBRARY
MOUNT MARY COLLEGE
MILWAUKEE, WISCONSIN 53222

WITHDRAWN

The We-Force in Management

How to Build and Sustain Cooperation

Lawrence G. Hrebiniak

LEXINGTON BOOKS
An Imprint of Macmillan, Inc.
NEW YORK

Maxwell Macmillan Canada
TORONTO

Maxwell Macmillan International
NEW YORK   OXFORD   SINGAPORE   SYDNEY

Library of Congress Cataloging-in-Publication Data

Hrebiniak, Lawrence G.
    The we-force in management : how to build and sustain cooperation
/ Lawrence G. Hrebiniak.
        p.   cm.
    ISBN 0-02-915345-X : $24.95
    1. Work groups. 2. Communication in management. I. Title.
II. Title: How to build and sustain cooperation.
HD66.H73   1994
658.4'02—dc20   94-10294
                                                                    CIP

Copyright © 1994 by Lawrence G. Hrebiniak

An Imprint of Macmillan, Inc.

All rights reserved. No part of this book may be reproduced or transmitted
in any form or by any means, electronic or mechanical, including photocopying,
recording, or by any information storage and retrieval system, without permission
in writing from the Publisher.

Lexington Books
An Imprint of Macmillan, Inc.
866 Third Avenue, New York, N.Y. 10022

Maxwell Macmillan Canada, Inc.
1200 Eglinton Avenue East
Suite 200
Don Mills, Ontario, M3C 3N1

Macmillan, Inc. is part of the Maxwell Communication Group of Companies

Printed in the United States of America

printing number

1 2 3 4 5 6 7 8 9 10

658.4
H873w
1994

Contents

iii

Preface

Why aren't our organizations more effective or more profitable? We've been told that the causes of poor performance include being hamstrung by bureaucracy, overpowered by more nimble competitors, and challenged by change. While these and similar explanations have merit, I believe that an important root cause of poor performance is being overlooked: the inability to cooperate.

We find it very difficult to cooperate. Most managers—whether they work in a manufacturing company, bank, hospital, or government agency—would agree that our organizations would perform more effectively if cooperation were more widespread. We could generate more innovative ideas, provide better services, and keep customers happier if cooperation among strategic business units, functions, departments, and individuals were the rule rather than the exception. We'd be far better off if we fought with competitors in the marketplace as furiously as we compete internally for resources, recognition, and influence in our own organizations. Yet we don't cooperate very well. We'd rather compete than work together, even to the point of hurting company performance for individual gain.

Based on my experience of consulting with hundreds of managers in some of the world's best-known companies and my research in the area of strategy implementation, I have identified the major obstacles to cooperation. I also have developed guidelines to encourage cooperation. American companies have downsized, rightsized, reengineered, diversified, and managed for total quality. Now the urgent need is to cooperate. My work shows how to foster and sustain cooperation, despite potent forces against it.

There have been scores of good books on teamwork and groups, but this is not another. *The We-Force in Management* goes beyond teams or groups. Its scope is broader, encompassing the effects of organizational structure and geographical dispersion on cooperation. It considers cultural and individual factors that impede cooperation, as well as organization-wide incentives, coordination, and communication techniques that can foster cooperation. Developing a We-Force enhances collaboration among individuals, regional offices, teams, strategic business units, departments, and even joint venture and alliance partners.

I have made this book practical and action-oriented. Although the book is based on important research on organizations and management, my purpose is to be useful, not esoteric. The book directs its advice to middle- and upper-level managers who are concerned about the lack of cooperation in their companies. Discussions of obstacles to cooperation and the remedial steps needed to create and sustain it are intended for people who want to change their organizations in positive ways. By providing the concepts and methodology of the We-Force, I hope to spur readers to take needed action. *The We-Force in Management* contains answers—not always easy or quick solutions, but answers nonetheless for managers who seek to reap the benefits of cooperation so vitally needed in today's competitive global economy.

As one might expect, this book would have been impossible without the cooperation and effort of a number of key individuals. My friend and colleague Bill Joyce was an excellent sounding board for testing and clarifying of ideas and concepts. The bulk of the manuscript was typed by Elizabeth Moy, whose efforts, diligence, and good humor I appreciate. Beth Anderson, senior editor at Lexington Books, made many suggestions that immensely improved the manuscript and always offered her advice in a positive, helpful way. Finally, I would like to thank my wife, Donna, and son, Justin, who are not only extremely nice and cooperative people but who also understand the vagaries and shortcomings of professors and authors.

1

Whither Cooperation?

*Why can't we get our act together? /
Why is cooperation so vital?*

S ome U.S. businesses have stumbled badly and are still stumbling. As we've been told over and over again, something is fundamentally wrong with the way we work. Many have noted the serious, disquieting trends. By now, we all are painfully aware of:

- Declines in R&D expenditures
- Inefficient industries
- Poor quality of some products
- Decline in real wages
- Technological weaknesses in critical areas
- Slow response to market demands
- Loss of national and global markets
- And so on and so on

The underlying causes of these problems are many and complex. Some are clearly beyond the control of any single company or management. Certain causes are rooted in global economic and political forces that are difficult to change.

Yet managers do control some causes of our industrial and economic malaise. Efforts can make a difference in areas that are currently being ignored. Common practices, habits, or styles of management in our companies are producing or adding to many of the dire consequences being lamented.

In brief, many of our troubles are of our own making. They reflect

1

the results of management styles and attitudes that are not appropriate for the present or for an increasingly competitive future.

The Failure of Cooperation

A basic problem facing us is our inability to cooperate. Effective cooperation is the exception, not the rule in many companies. Managers talk about teamwork, but don't do it. They espouse cooperation and common goals, but then pursue their own individual interests. Cooperation, while vitally needed, is sacrificed at the alter of cutthroat competition and individual gain.

Is the inability or lack of desire to cooperate really a fundamental problem in our companies? I think it is, but don't take my word for it. Consider one recent discussion of the ills of U.S. industry—the Report of the MIT Commission on Industrial Productivity.

Among its findings is a serious observation: the failure of cooperation within U.S. companies. The effects of this failure are clear: Poor cooperation impedes innovation. Poor coordination and cooperation result in slow or deficient product design and development. Poor communication across functions, strategic business units (SBUs), and other structural "silos" hurts joint ventures and cooperative efforts. Poor cooperation and coordination result in slow response to market changes and technological developments.

I personally can underscore these findings. In my research and consulting work with executives, I have observed the same painful and disquieting lack of cooperation in many companies and its adverse impacts on quality, innovation, and competitive strength. Other issues get more attention in the business press, such as recession, debt, trade deficits, global competition, interest rates, restructurings, and so on. But it is our increasing inability to cooperate, to work together, that ought to alarm us. Listen to just one manager at an executive program I ran recently:

> Damn it, the basic problem is with us. We do strategic planning and competitive analysis. We identify the external bad guys, the foreign competitors who are causing us major grief in our markets. So, what do we do?
>
> Hell, we do nothing about the competition. We're too wrapped up in fighting with each other! We're all trying to look good. We hurt

each other to look good. We'd kill each other for more resources and for the inside track to the top guys. Score is not being kept on how we do as a company, but on how I do, how good I look, how good my SBU is evaluated by the execs. To tell you the truth, I sometimes think we're stupid. I sometimes think we're in big trouble.

Confronting the Problem

Why is cooperation vital to competitive success? The world is changing, demanding more in terms of joint efforts within companies. We are all familiar with the characteristics of the new business environment.

Global competition is here to stay. Competing effectively globally demands sharing and effective coordination. Core competence often must be leveraged across business units to maximize benefit from skills and company strengths. SBUs and other business units cannot remain islands or fiefdoms, but must learn to cooperate and derive maximum return and leverage from scarce resources across country boundaries. Global competition also creates the occasional need for joint ventures, strategic alliances, and similar forms of cooperation to allow companies to enter and effectively compete in foreign markets.

Managing our companies is becoming more complex. More than ever, lateral coordination and cooperation across functions are critical to product development and customer satisfaction. Complex organizational structures—for example, matrix organizations—intensify coordination and communication problems. The need for speed in responding to markets demands greater teamwork and sharing of responsibilities. Attempts at restructuring or reengineering the corporation cannot succeed without attention to lateral activities, processes, and information flows, all of which depend on cooperation and coordination across diverse units or functions.

Mature, more competitive markets are the rule, not the exception. Yesterday's expanding frontiers demanded rugged individuals to conquer new territories. Many markets are more mature now, and winning is more difficult. Winning often involves taking from established competitors, in contrast to everyone gaining in an expanding, high-growth market with plenty to go around. Competing under mature, even declining conditions, demands more teamwork and sharing of skills.

More than ever, companies must attend to external threats. Many companies are in a fight for their lives. It's time to stop fighting within companies and focus, instead, on action against our real competitive opponents.

Fleshing Out a Problem

More than ever, we need cooperation and what it creates or brings to an organization, including unity of direction, purposeful coordination, leveraging of core competence, and a sense of teamwork. Effective cooperation suggests decision making directed toward superordinate goals, not just individual benefit or gain. It represents joint effort and effective communication among those engaged in a task.

Cooperative systems do not exist in many U.S. companies. Instead, injurious competition dwarfs cooperation. Win-lose battles are commonplace, detracting from cooperative effort. Emphasis is on individual achievement, reward, and recognition, not on superordinate goals. Managers talk a good game about participation, joint decision making, risk-taking, and interdependence, but their actions and apparent motivations belie their talk.

What prevailing conditions preclude the development and sustenance of cooperation as a pervasive force among managers? My research and experience have identified a number of debilitating barriers to cooperation.

Emphasis on the short term. The short term rules most American managers. They talk about long-term and strategic issues but usually focus on short-run costs and profitability. Strategic needs are mortgaged for short-term gains. Cooperation often demands a longer-term or strategic emphasis, but managers' attention to short-term performance and quick rewards is often inconsistent with a long-term, integrative view.

Managers are motivated as individuals. Reward systems in most companies recognize only individual performance. Rewards foster individual hedonism, not joint, cooperative efforts. Getting ahead is critical, even if occasionally it's at the expense of the larger good. Managers say "we" or "us" but act out "I."

Tying this observation back to the previous point, behavior is often directed toward immediate gratification rather than longer-term, strategic needs. From the boardroom to the factory locker-room, concern is with the here-and-now, not with the long haul. The need for immediate feedback and rewards motivates short-term thinking and predominantly individual concerns, not cooperative effort directed toward common goals.

Superordinate goals sound good but have little impact on mangers' actions. Mission statements and strategic plans are loaded with euphemisms and elegant statements about the importance of shareholder value, long-term growth, the centrality of consumer needs, and the team efforts required to meet lofty goals. However, individual goals and needs prevail. Working together for superordinate goals is fine, as long as joint efforts don't take too much time and effort away from more important individual concerns.

We build barriers to cooperation. A host of things get in the way of cooperation, and many of them are of our own doing. Organizational structure creates hurdles for teamwork and barriers to effective communication. Organizations like SBUs are created to promote flexibility and a market focus, but lead to turf battles and fights for resources. Control systems bias feedback and information. Performance appraisal often pits manager against manager, unit against unit, thus dividing the organization.

Organizational cultures hurt cooperation. High levels of distrust among managers caused by the restructurings and mass white-collar layoffs of the early 1990s are encouraging competition and cynicism. More than ever, emphasis in many companies is on "looking out for number one," not on sharing ideas and working together to improve overall performance.

A Time for Action and Change

This diagnosis sounds pretty bleak; however, we *can* do something about it. Managers tell me they want to change, and I believe them. What, then, is necessary for change to occur? There are two central aspects to effective change and the creation of cooperation.

First, we must recognize the obstacles to cooperation. Some of the obstacles to effective cooperation are fairly well known, but others are not. Some obstacles are endemic to a particular culture or country, while others are more widespread, affecting cooperation in companies throughout the world. Before any cure can be effected, it is imperative to know and fully undersand what's preventing the creation and use of cooperative systems and ventures.

Second, the steps necessary to create and sustain cooperation must be spelled out. Managers need to develop a method to help them generate cooperation. They need to know the steps or actions that foster cooperation and overcome the obstacles to it.

This book addresses these two interdependent issues. It focuses on how to build and sustain cooperation. It answers the play-on-words title of this chapter: where has cooperation gone in many companies or, alternatively, why it has withered in importance.

Most importantly, this book focuses pragmatically on steps managers in all companies can take to improve cooperation and teamwork. It shows how individual, group, and overall organizational factors can coalesce, not to destroy cooperation but to affect it positively. The chapters that follow discuss strategic and operating conditions and topics not normally linked to teamwork. Toward this end, I discuss three essential concepts.

The *I-Force*. This term refers to the predominantly individualistic nature of American managers. It represents a strong need for individual achievement and success, a motivation that drives competitive behavior.

The I-Force helped create an aggressive, successful, capitalistic America. But at the current stage of U.S. economic development, the I-Force is also leading managers to avoid interdependence and to work against cooperative systems. I argue that the positive aspects of the I-Force must be harnessed to create a critical new thrust, the "We-Force."

Barriers to cooperation. In addition to the I-Force, other barriers impede effective cooperation. Many of these obstacles are not characteristically American but are common to companies globally. Organizational conditions and forces present additional formidable obstacles. These include, but are not limited to: organizational structure, geographical dispersion of operating units, incentive plans that militate against cooperation, performance appraisal and review methods that foster destructive competition, and control or feedback systems that do not reinforce cooperative efforts. These obstacles are commonplace and often debilitating, but they can be overcome to create a We-Force.

The We-Force. The We-Force emphasizes cooperation. It is

founded on interdependence and the need for joint decision making. It focuses attention on agreement and superordinate goals. The We-Force facilitates communication and coordination, and helps managers appreciate problems in other parts of an organization or in the company as a whole. Emphasis of the We-Force, then, is on systems thinking and on an appreciation of how multiple forces exist and interact to affect cooperation.

The methodology for creating cooperation is logical, practical, and doable. Success provides clear benefits, both for the company and the managers involved. The We-Force represents a win-win situation in which the company gains and managers become much more effective in their jobs.

In the following chapters I discuss these and related issues. My goal is to help the reader understand the obstacles to cooperation and the steps that can be taken to create and nurture it.

2

Barriers to Cooperation

*The I-Force / The Lone Ranger
phenomenon / Organizational forces that
work against cooperation*

*In this company, people have always worked alone together. The same
question comes up time and time again when discussing new projects:
"What's in it for me?"*

*The corporate culture is that big dogs eat little dogs. And the size of
your meal is determined by one thing only—your individual numbers.*

*Cooperation? Forget it! It's too hard getting past the barbed wire and
machine guns to even talk to people on other projects, much less work
closely with them. Stars get ahead around here, not constellations.*

This chapter explains why managers like those just quoted feel
as they do. It explores individual and organizational barriers to
effective communication and cooperation.

Individual Barriers to Cooperation:
The Pervasive I-Force

Culture affects cooperation and competition. It predisposes individuals to work together or separately to achieve their purposes. In
certain Eastern cultures, people routinely strive for harmony and
cooperation and avoid conflict and direct confrontation at all costs.
The different cultures within Europe affect the way the Italians,
Germans, French, and Swiss do business.

Along these lines, there is a need or motivation common to managers in U.S. companies. This tendency forces attention on individual performance and calls for personal recognition. It often detracts from cooperative behavior and effective communication. I call this pervasive and important drive the I-Force, short for Individual Force. The I-Force is a logical starting point in understanding how cultural and individual forces predispose U.S. managers against cooperation and joint effort.

The Protestant Ethic

While the I-Force cannot be explained fully by any single cause or set of conditions, an important starting point in understanding it is the work done by the great sociologist Max Weber, who identified what he called the Protestant Ethic.[1] Weber's research links the rise of capitalism to a religious and cultural ethic, and he shows how the frugality and individualism underlying this ethic provided the basis for economic growth.

An important doctrine considered by Weber is predestination, which marked Calvinism and other early religious beliefs in Europe. Simply stated, this doctrine meant that people cannot control whether they go to heaven or hell. A person's fate is predetermined. A person who spends a lifetime doing all sorts of good deeds cannot be sure of the ultimate result. The outcome—salvation or infinite pain—is predetermined at the time of conception. People live their lives with the final conclusion already written, signed, and sealed in the heavenly record.

Predestination forged a uniquely individualistic perspective. Concerns about heaven are obviously personal, not matters of group control. Individuals go to heaven or hell, not families, groups, or committees. In the final analysis, each person worried about himself or herself first and foremost. Eternity, after all, is a long time!

Understandably, this inevitability of outcome could make people extremely anxious. Although they couldn't alter their destinies, people felt compelled to do something to get a glimpse of their fates. One response was to look for signs from heaven, suggestions that one must be among the chosen. A farmer or merchant doing well, for example, could interpret his bounty or economic success as a positive sign of heavenly predestination. Things were going well because God takes care of his chosen disciples.

But what if things were not going well? If locusts ravaged the farmer's crops or the merchant found his business foundering, was this an inevitable sign of eternal damnation? Was bad fortune a sign that everything was going to hell, literally?

No, even if things were not going well, one should never give up. The trials and tribulations merely could be a heavenly test of one's mettle and resolve. Overcoming major adversities and problems on earth could elevate one's status among the chosen. The message was clear: hard work and persistence would pay off! Thus, whether the signs from heaven were positive or negative, the religious ethic advocated hard work and continued industriousness.

There is more to the religious ideology than hard work and persistence, however. There is also a motivation for investment and growth, which clearly represent the seeds of capitalism.

Consider the successful farmer or merchant whose crops were plentiful or whose business was booming. Profits were high. Hard work and commitment to the task as a labor of religious zeal produced strong positive results.

What should the farmer or merchant do with excess profits? Certainly, many options were categorically ruled out. The profits could not be spent on excessive revelry or debauchery, for example, because such activities were considered sinful and inconsistent with the centrality of work and good deeds in one's life.

Two acceptable actions came to the fore. They were: (1) donate a portion of the profits to the church, and (2) reinvest the acquired capital back into the farm or business. Success of the farm or business, after all, was thought to be symbolic of one's predetermined lot in the afterlife. Continued success would confirm one's positive fate, so it was wise to invest and grow to continue to curry heaven's favor.

Thus, the Protestant Ethic was characterized by hard work; a commitment to the task; never giving up, even when confronted with poor performance or work-related problems; a sense of frugality and self-denial; and a need to reinvest accumulated earnings to achieve growth. Weber argued that these basic forces and underlying motivations sparked the rise of capitalism.

The religious ethic described by Weber began in Europe but gradually spread. People coming to the New World brought their motivations and religious zeal with them. Early settlers to what was to become the United States were characterized by a commitment to work, frugality, investment, and growth.

Over time, the religious trappings or connections became less salient and were diluted by other aspects of culture and social adaptation. Still, a cultural ethic, if not a religious one, remained. American culture slowly but surely was imbued with the concept of virtues of hard work, frugality, and growth. When Benjamin Franklin and others offered wisdom about the prudence of saving pennies, the benefits of work, the dangers of being borrowers or lenders, and the sure-fire negative consequences of idle minds, they were reflecting this underlying cultural bias or ethic.

In this way, the seeds of the I-Force were planted. Cultural emphasis on hard work, investment, and individual achievement provided the needed fertilizer for growth and strength. The rise of capitalism and entrepreneurship in the United States at the hands of people like Edison, Whitney, Ford, Carnegie, and Rockefeller both reflected and nurtured this intense individual drive to grow and succeed.

Of most significance to us presently, managers in this culture were driven by a need for individual success. Researchers over time have reported evidence supporting this emphasis on personal achievement and the strength of an I-Force. The noted psychologist David McClelland, for example, found in his ground-breaking research that:[2]

- U.S. managers have a strong drive to succeed and a high need for achievement.
- Managers feel a need to differentiate their own performance from that of their peers.
- Managers are motivated to work and contribute as individuals.
- Success is measured and rewards determined by performance against individual goals.

I-Force—The Backlash?

Unquestionably the I-Force has had a major positive impact on individuals, organizations, and entire economies. At the individual level, one reward lies in the *intrinsic* feedback and satisfaction that come with successfully completing a task. Achievement simply feels good.

Related to intrinsic satisfaction is the *extrinsic* feedback that accompanies success. Companies reward individuals who produce. The hard work, commitment, and time that produce positive outcomes for a company do not go unnoticed. Salary, promotion, and perquisites are usually associated with good performance.

The individualistic drives of the I-Force can also produce positive results for the organizations that employ such motivated people. Organizations can be seen as cooperative systems, directed toward the achievement of agreed-upon goals. The collective purpose clearly must be consistent with the purpose, needs, or goals of the individuals who comprise the system. If this consistency is achieved, the motivations, ambitions, and drives of individual performers will add up to positive organizational outcomes.

In essence, consistency of goals results in a win-win situation. A business wins (increased profits, market share) when its individuals perform and also win (promotion, salary, bonus). If there is no divergence between the common good and the goals of individuals comprising the collective unit, all is consistent and well and the I-Force positively affects company performance.

It follows logically, too, that entire countries can also benefit from the I-Force. A nation of individuals with a strong work ethic clearly should outperform other nations with no such ethic. Indeed, research has shown that this common-sense notion is true.

McClelland, for example, has shown a clear relationship between a work ethic or need for achievement and the level of productivity within countries. An analysis of different countries' books and songs that measured the achievement-related themes showed that achievement drives are positively related to economic success. In 1925, Britain ranked fifth among twenty-five countries when children's readers were scored for achievement needs. By the 1950s the level of achievement themes in those readers had dropped to twenty-seventh out of thirty-nine countries, coinciding with the economic decline of that nation.

These studies have also looked at the literatures of ancient Greece, Spain, and other countries and found that when their literature reflected the theme of achievement and the values of the work ethic, the countries performed well economically. In the United States, the rags-to-riches stories of Horatio Alger both reflected and affected a drive to get ahead. Alger's heroes were always striving; they were honest, cheerful, industrious role models for Americans in the last third of the nineteenth century, an unprecedented era of growth in the United States.

The I-Force helped make the United States great, a world leader in economic growth and industrial innovation. At the present time, however, the United States is suffering. And the I-Force, paradoxically, may be partly to blame. I emphasize the partly, for rarely is the answer to any complex problem as simplistic as blaming a single cause or variable. Still, the I-Force is having some negative, if unintended, consequences for performance, primarily in its adverse impact on cooperation and teamwork within companies. Let's consider why this may be the case today.

In the early stages of a country's economic growth , the I-Force clearly is beneficial. The expansion of the United States into uncharted areas, for example, obviously demanded an aggressive, competitive people. Indeed, the original European settlers must have been risk-takers, driven by a need to escape persecution and achieve growth and success in the New World.

Similarly, in new or emerging industries, the I-Force is a positive influence. Risk taking and innovation are needed to develop new technologies, markets, and production standards. Competitive, aggressive managers are vital to the forging of strategic thrusts under uncertain conditions, with no guarantees of success.

However, today the growth curve in many industries and countries is at a more mature stage. While innovation and entrepreneurship are always vital, the more mature and competitive U.S. and world economies increasingly are demanding cooperation and the sharing of skills and technology. Joint ventures and cooperative alliances are more common as companies attempt to share expensive R&D efforts and avoid constantly reinventing the wheel in the areas of technology and expensive distribution systems. If the I-Force militates against the needed cooperation, negative results may ensue.

Consider global competition, which often requires a company to compete worldwide in a coordinated, controlled way. Comparative advantage derived in one location must be leveraged to provide competitive advantage in other places in the world. Similarly, a company's core competence or set of scarce skills in one area must be shared to allow a positive competitive position elsewhere. Coordination and cooperation, then, are vital to global strategic success. Cooperation, however, can be an elusive commodity.

Let me give an actual example. A well-known company that competes globally in both consumer and industrial markets has product divisions for worldwide competition, as well as regional and country managers to maintain a local presence. The individual country managers are charged with the task of determining the best product mix to ensure growth of the company in their particular countries. Such a manager might need only certain products from the company's different divisions to optimize locally. Product line managers, in contrast, are charged with pushing the entire line worldwide, in all countries.

Here is a situation made either for conflict or beneficial cooperation. While working with the country manager, the product line manager may realize that another division's line of products may be better for the country's markets. Another product line may secure a better competitive position for the company as a global entity. Does the product line manager push only his or her own products to the country manager, despite knowing that other lines are better for the country in question? Or does this manager suggest the other lines, knowing that local competitive advantage and the company's overall position and goals are better served by them?

Clearly, cooperation and joint decision making are better for the company. However, the individualistic nature of the I-Force and the company's reward system can work against the needed cooperation. If both managers perceive a win-win situation, the cooperation and coordination so vital to global competition will occur. If individual drives and the supporting reward structure emphasize a win-lose situation, cooperation will not occur. In fact, managers may take advantage of others to get ahead, even though superordinate company goals are hurt.

Perhaps by now many of you are thinking the same things expressed by some of the people I knew in the company: "How naive you are. Faced with the situation just described, a product line manager obviously will push his own products. No one in his right mind would suggest the products of other divisions, even if that situation were optimal for the company and country alike." "C'mon, grow up! You know damn well what's going to happen here. The product manager is going to do what's best for himself. Period. Done."

If you feel this way, I agree with your assessment of the situation. I know how most managers would act. This is exactly the point I'm striving to make.

The need for individual achievement is so strongly ingrained in most managers that concerns for cooperative efforts and superordinate goals rather than personal benefit rarely even enter into the decision. Cooperative effort is all right as long as it doesn't detract from individual performance, recognition, and reward. "Teamwork is fine, as long as I'm recognized," to quote one of the company's product line managers pointedly. He later added, "preferably recognized *more* than the other guys."

The I-Force has been and still can be a positive force in U.S. companies, and I'm certainly not recommending that we try to extinguish it. The real issue is how to control and direct the I-Force into positive outcomes for a company. The critical task is to build upon and positively use strong individual drives to create a culture that nurtures a We-Force—systems of cooperation directed toward superordinate goals. Before tackling this issue, however, we need to identify organizational barriers to cooperation that may be related to the I-Force.

The I-Force and Organizational Barriers to Cooperation

INCENTIVE SYSTEMS

One of the strongest perpetuators of the I-Force is the reward system. This observation should not be surprising, for incentive systems, after all, are created by and cater to individuals with strong needs for achievement and personal recognition. "Teamwork" sounds good, but doesn't feed the dog or pay the bills. Cooperation is a holy word and, when uttered, managers aptly nod in agreement, like toy dogs in the rear windows of cars. But, too often, these same managers immediately go off and behave in a singularly individualistic fashion. The simple fact is that, in most companies:

- Base salary depends on individual performance. Payment rarely, if ever, increases primarily as a direct result of cooperation.
- Promotion is also an individual reward. Groups don't get ahead, individuals do. So why get involved in joint or cooperative ventures that blur individual achievement?
- Bonuses usually are tied to SBU, division, or product line perfor-

mance—that is, to individual units within the larger company. If division managers can increase their returns on investment and their bonuses, even at the expense of another part of the company, they often are tempted to do so.

- Although stock options for higher-level managers seem to focus on the good of the whole company, these options can be manipulated to foster individual gain. A drop in the stock price, for example, is usually met by a lowering of the price at which managers can exercise the option. Thus individuals win regardless of stock performance. And even when they exercise the option, managers rarely remain owners. Rather, they cash in for individual gain, perhaps thinking not of the company and other shareholders but, rather, of something like a nice sailboat in Tahiti.

Because of these factors, organizational reward systems and incentives motivate and reinforce individual performance, thus impeding cooperation and, ultimately, company performance.

SHORT-TERM THINKING

When the emphasis is on individual gratification, there is a tendency to shorten the time horizon for action and feedback. Long-term results are too distant to reinforce behavior. One line manager's comments echo the thoughts of many others: "Let the high-priced folks in corporate strategic planning worry about the long haul. I'm getting paid to put out fires and make things work today."

Companies, of course, need "fire fighters," or crisis managers. The danger arises when short-term thinking dominates organizational culture at the expense of long-term or strategic thinking. Unfortunately, short-term thinking is reinforced throughout most organizations. Several individual and organizational factors conspire against long-term planning:

- Performance appraisal systems in companies reinforce the short term. Strategic performance indicators rarely, if ever, share importance with short-term measures in the evaluation process.
- Fast-track managers expect promotions and new job assignments every two or three years, despite costly interruptions to the work or projects they leave behind.
- Wall Street analysts make short-term performance, like quarterly earnings, extremely salient. Shareholders or owners more often

than not are large institutional investors looking for quick returns in their portfolios, so they further emphasize short-run performance and thinking.
• Normal company culture applauds the manager who is decisive and quick to make decisions, not the long-term thinker.

All of these common tendencies cater to immediate and individual fulfillment, to the detriment of cooperation.

THE NOT-INVENTED-HERE SYNDROME

The NIH (not invented here) syndrome is a clear symptom of the I-Force and one cause of the demise of cooperative effort. Simply stated, the work of people in different functions, divisions, and departments is ignored because "I can do it better." The logic is that we know our own problems, so we are the best people to design solutions to them. What's invented by us is good; what comes from others won't work. This syndrome helps create companies in which people work alone together, thereby frustrating innovation and cooperation. There are two explanations for the NIH syndrome.

First, emphasis on individual achievement breeds egoistical thinking. What I do (or what someone like me does) is clearly the best. I therefore reject the work of other individuals, functions, or groups in the company. These people are not like me and cannot do things as well as I can. In the extreme, this attitude leads to a myth of omnipotence, a debilitating situation in which individuals feel that their superior knowledge logically allows them to reject the authority, influence, and insights of all others.

The second reason is related to the competition for recognition among high achievers. Again, individual achievement, recognition, and promotion are valued in most companies. What happens, then, when someone else does something well or wishes to cooperate on a joint venture? By accepting the help, I may be admitting that on my own I cannot accomplish the same thing. The cooperative contract suggests that individuals in the helping group are somehow better than the individuals in the accepting group. Or individuals in one group may fear that they can make others look good in some way, thereby intensifying competition for recognition. If this upside-down logic prevails, NIH and a lack of cooperation will be the norm.

NIH dysfunctions are frequently based on I-Force thinking. Poor communication, coordination, and cooperation are very likely to be related to individual needs and motivations.

Additional Organizational Obstacles

Other organizational factors affecting cooperation are not directly attributable to personality or individual needs. These obstacles are found in companies all over the world. A good example of such a common or pervasive obstacle is organizational structure.

Organizational Structure

The way a company is organized can have a profound effect on communication, coordination, and cooperation. Consider one simple example, the common functional organization (see figure 2.1).

There are benefits to a functional structure. It is simple to understand and divides responsibilities into clear categories. Efficiency or scale economies result from high volume and repetitive, standardized efforts within functions, such as production. Control is often enhanced via centralized, uniform responsibility, as in finance or marketing.

But division into functions also creates perceptual differences and turf battles. Many years ago I heard a manufacturing manager complaining about his counterpart in marketing: "There's no stopping this guy—he'll do anything for a sale. He'll promise the customer all sorts of things, including unrealistic modifications [to the products]. Why the hell can't he sell what we make?!"

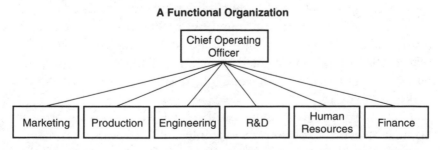

Figure 2.1

When I voiced manufacturing's concerns to the person in sales and marketing, his response was hardly surprising. "That's typical of him. All he cares about are long productions runs. If he could, he'd put the whole world in a one-pound jar. Why can't he be more flexible? Why the hell can't he make what we sell?!"

The point is that they both were right. Each function sees the world differently. The training, preparation, and job responsibilities in each area are different. Salespeople are paid to sell, and manufacturing people are paid to produce lots of things at low cost.

In some cases, this functional myopia is so strong that managers in one function cannot understand, appreciate, or value the work in other functions. It prevents managers from seeing the big picture or what the entire company is all about. When a manufacturing company I worked with lost a major customer, the organization did not want to get together to find out what had gone wrong. Instead, finger-pointing and blame-finding were the norm.

And, of course, the blame was not with us but with them: "Hell, I don't know what happened. All I know is that the engineering specs were OK. We did our job, despite their wanting to change the damn design every other day. We did our part, so don't blame us. *They* (manufacturing, marketing, etc.) screwed up somehow. Better find out what *they* did before this happens again."

Care to guess *their* reaction when engineering's charges were related in this case? Care to guess who became the *they* who really screwed up?

As bad as this situation was, it only got worse. Functional myopia and finger-pointing caused problems of coordination, communication, and cooperation, which only increased the possibilities of additional performance problems. These problems lead to more finger-pointing and blaming, which further damaged cooperation. The vicious cycle continued, with each function remaining holier-than-thou as yet one more big customer sought service elsewhere. "Don't ask me what's wrong! I just know that the problem's not here. We're doing our job, despite the others trying to make us look bad."

The same type of problem can be seen when looking at other popular structural forms—for example, SBUs. The SBU is a separate, discrete business unit that focuses on a particular market, product, or customer. The SBU usually enjoys autonomy and is often self-contained and minimally dependent, if at all, on other SBUs.

The SBU usually competes with other SBUs for resources. The corporate parent evaluates all the businesses and decides where investment is most beneficial. When resources are scarce, this competition can be intense, even counterproductive.

If each SBU is trying to out-do the others to gain and hoard resources, cooperation is at risk. Secrets, technologies, innovations, skills, and resources will not be not shared. It's better to keep good things within the SBU so as to maintain advantage over the others. Cooperation and potential synergies die as each SBU become a vertical silo, keeping to itself rather than sharing for the overall good of the company.

The point is not to condemn structure; organization is necessary and important. Rather, the point is to show that structure can create barriers to communication and cooperation. Structure separates or differentiates and can create turf battles, competition, and conflicting perceived job responsibilities. Geographical dispersion of structural units makes coordination and communication even more problematical. These factors make the definition and resolution of common problems almost impossible. Cooperation can not be improved without recognizing and resolving the ways the organizational structure acts as a potential barrier.

Business or Functional Strategies

Although well-formulated strategies provide many benefits to companies, they also can inhibit cooperation. For example, marketing strategy views getting close to customers and providing high-quality service as critical. Manufacturing sees its strategy a bit differently, aiming for a cost leadership position and the volume, standardization, and efficiency that role implies.

Are these strategies and the goals or activities they suggest consistent? In many cases, yes. But strategic orientations can become so differentiated that performance can suffer. A cost leadership strategy in one part of the company can negatively affect the quest for quality or good service in another unit that sees the need to differentiate itself from competition.

It took months before we finally got a break with [a customer]. Months of hard work, promises, and a tough selling job. We finally convinced them that our system would perform even better than the one provided by [a major competitor].

So, what happens? I'll tell you! We ship the stuff, they try it, and tell us it's no damn good! Doesn't meet their quality tests. Doesn't perform up to specs. The quality isn't there.

Do you know what happened? I'll tell you. Manufacturing's been on this low-cost kick. Without telling us, they've been substituting cheaper materials in what they call noncritical components. Trouble is, that's not what the customer calls them. The bastards cut their costs, but they hurt the product. More importantly, they hurt our credibility with customers. If the word gets out on this, we're screwed royally.

Cases like this are more common than we'd like to admit. A drive for a performance goal in one part of a company can hurt another part of the same company. One function's meat truly is another's poison.

In other cases, one department may question another department's value, or even whether it should exist. Consider R&D and the operating divisions of a company. The operating divisions concentrate on the here and now, in real time, putting out fires, serving customers, and generating short-term revenues and profits. This is where the rubber meets the road, so to speak.

In contrast, as a manager in an automotive company once expressed it, R&D is "where the rubber meets the sky!" R&D usually has a long-term view. Its work is often seen as playing, or experimenting with new ideas. R&D personnel may be seen as dilettantes who take away from current earnings, but who rarely give anything back. These beliefs about value-added and the relative contributions of functional strategies can clearly affect perceptions and behavior, including cooperative efforts.

Different functional or business strategies often require people of varying skills, education, and experience. An advanced engineering group responsible for R&D and major product innovations will have job requirements different from those found in administrative or accounting departments. But differences in job tenure, skills, responsibilities, and experience can affect communication and cooperation. For example, companies hire young, aggressive, MBA-types from places like Wharton for positions in strategic planning. These new employees are well-versed in computer skills and the quantitative decision sciences. They like to play with different models, algorithms, and programs. They pursue sophisticated planning methods, not those based on simple heuristics or rules-of-thumb.

The line managers responsible for the implementation of the plans, on the other hand, are usually older, with longer job tenure but less formal education than the strategists. They occasionally brag about their experience on the job and their graduation from the school of hard knocks. The line managers may not understand the planners' efforts. They may even see the plans as quantitative mumbo-jumbo from the minds of kids who really don't understand the business or the industry.

The bottom line is that the planners and doers are completely different. The older, experienced line people don't understand the strategic planning process or the resultant plans, but they won't seek clarification from "kids still wet behind the ears." Rather than trying to understand the plans, the doers ignore or criticize the planners and their output. The planners, in turn, assume an air of arrogance and disdain for those they perceive as cretins who refuse to be educated on twenty-first century methods. And so it goes.

If such differences in tenure, experience, or job responsibility persist between groups whose tasks are highly interdependent, cooperation will suffer dramatically.

Competitive Company Cultures

Culture is another company characteristic that reflects and affects values, missions, modus operandi, and acceptable competitive behavior

As already suggested, the culture of many organizations is dominated by competition. There is competition to be recognized and get ahead. There is competition for scarce resources, power, and control over critical decisions. To be sure, competition has a plus side for companies. Competition enables the company to pick and choose from among options developed by good people trying their hardest to produce. Competition within companies, as within industries, forces those competing to remain sharp and up to date.

However, competition also can wear a negative face. It can breed a win-lose mentality within a company and motivate people to make sure they win and avoid the stigma of losing. But winning at all costs and ensuring that others lose can be divisive. A company culture in which it's "every man for himself" creates distrust, back-stabbing, and other barriers to cooperation.

Competition for scarce resources can also lead to serious dysfunctions. Individuals, departments, and divisions routinely seek a larger share of available resources. They may even try to keep others from getting too much of the resource pie. Units may hoard resources to keep them away from competing units that, after all, could look too good if they had the resources on hand. The impact on cooperation is obvious.

A caveat is in order. A competitive culture does not necessarily injure or destroy cooperation. It is possible to harness what's good or beneficial in competition and focus it on positive company outcomes. Similarly, the destructive side of intense competition can be controlled, if not totally exorcised from a company, so as to create a more positive climate for cooperative behavior.

Power and Politics.

The quest for power or increased influence is a given in most companies. But the drive for power or influence and the behavior it implies can affect cooperation. Consider a simple definition of power. Assume two company units or functions, A & B. A has power over B in direct proportion to A's having something B needs. A's power is also related to the ability to monopolize what B needs. If A has something B sorely needs, and B cannot get it elsewhere, B is totally dependent on A. Conversely, A has a great amount of power or influence over B. Power is the opposite of dependency.

This is a broad notion of power, but it is useful because it describes influence at different levels of analysis—individuals, groups, organizations, and countries. Power issues appear constantly, as the following examples suggest.

"OK. If I do this for you, what's in it for me?" The manager here is exercising her influence and demanding something in return for her effort. The suggestion is that she might withhold her effort if a suitable incentive is not offered for it.

"I need [an internal supplier]. I can't buy these components outside, so he has me over a barrel. He controls my production. How can I do good work when that S.O.B. gives me nothing or sends me junk?" Vertical integration creates dependencies that occasionally result in conflicts over power and control, as this manager's comments indicate.

Power as the opposite of dependency is a useful concept because it relates nicely to the issue of cooperation and joint decision making. Cooperation implies interdependence or mutual dependence in task-related matters. Skills or expertise in organizational units must be used or shared by others. Cooperation suggests this sharing. It also implies a norm of reciprocity, as organizational units give and get something in a series of exchanges to achieve company goals.

Our definition of power, however, does not suggest a norm of reciprocity and mutual dependence. It argues that A will do everything possible to make B dependent and to keep that dependency unilateral. It suggests that A will resist becoming dependent on B to avoid vulnerability to B. If power is the opposite of dependency, then the quest for power suggests an avoidance of mutual dependence, reciprocity, and cooperation.

If organizations are seen as cooperative systems focused on common goals, then this notion of power reveals serious problems. In an extreme case, everyone in the organization is focusing selfishly on garnering resources to create dependencies. The goal is to control key resources and get power, even if this pursuit hurts someone else. Under these circumstances, there is little motivation to share resources or core skills and technology, and the drive to tackle superordinate issues that benefit others diminishes over time. Emphasis, again, is on I rather than on we, as wholesale jockeying for critical resources to form a base of power becomes the norm. These conditions can only hurt cooperation, teamwork, and shared decision making.

Throughout this chapter, I've argued that there are formidable barriers to cooperative efforts. Basic motivational forces and organizational factors seem to support and nurture self-serving, individualistic, uncooperative behavior. Can anything be done to foster a We-Force—shared responsibilities, joint efforts, and cooperation directed at superordinate goals? The following chapters take up this critical question, beginning with an elaboration of the We-Force.

3

The We-Force

*What is the We-Force? / How does it benefit
managers and their companies?*

What the We-Force Isn't

B efore talking about what the We-Force is, let us consider what
is not meant or implied by the term. My purpose here simply is
to avoid misunderstanding that could inhibit implementation of
We-Force thinking.

The We-Force is not socialism. It does not advocate or foster centralized goal setting within a company. It doesn't suggest that individual contributions lose importance or that a central source unilaterally determines plans, ideas, and actions.

The We-Force does *not attempt to negate or eliminate the I-Force.*
As already shown, the I-Force is too ingrained in U.S. managers and
can have positive outcomes. Strong individual motivations in other
cultures can have similar beneficial effects. The We-Force, as we shall
see, does attempt to better control individual actions for the attainment of superordinate goals. While the I-Force is pervasive and valuable, care must be taken to avoid its negative and divisive effects.

The We-Force isn't *touchy-feely or wishy-washy.* It isn't a catchy
gimmick or fad in the same way that the I-Force hasn't been and
isn't a gimmick or fad. The concepts and techniques of the We-Force are not limited to certain levels, functions, or parts of a company. The methodology needed to attain the We-Force and the cooperation it entails is logical, rigorous, and capable of making
significant contributions to company performance.

The methodology for cooperation and teamwork does *not hurt individual managers or make them less effective.* Overall, the steps necessary to create and sustain cooperation are beneficial to management development and to the improvement, not the deterioration, of management skills.

The required techniques, insights, and skills *are not industry specific* but apply to all organizations and industries. The We-Force methodology is effective and useful in nonprofit and for-profit institutions, including both manufacturing and service industries.

The We-Force is *not limited to the use of teams or groups.* It is not a synonym for team organization. Certainly, the We-Force often relies on groups or teams, but it goes beyond the group concept. SBU managers, for example, consistent with the We-Force, may strive for superordinate corporate goals without ever formally joining or forming a team for coordinated cooperative effort. They serve the common good without being bound in a group setting. The We-Force, then, does not always denote people routinely working together and interacting face-to-face.

The basic tenets and concepts underlying the We-Force are not new, but they are somewhat revolutionary. They and their logic have been ignored or buried deep beneath managers' thresholds of thought and action because of the individual concerns spawned by the I-Force over time.

I-Force Versus We-Force

This company doesn't exist first and foremost for shareholders. Company goals include a fair return to owners, and a fair shake for customers, suppliers, and others, but all of this is of secondary importance. The *prime* beneficiaries of company performance, the real winners, are the managers in this room here today. The primary reason for working for this company is to maintain the good life, *our* good life.

This statement was made by the director of strategic planning of a Fortune 500 company, who delivered it behind closed doors as part of a sermon to believing members of the flock, to be sure. Obviously, not everyone reading this book concurs with his point. At least, not many managers would admit it so freely.

This opinion reflects, in the extreme, the strong individual needs and self-centered aspects of the I-Force. It raises pertinent questions about superordinate goals and the real beneficiaries of corporate purpose and action. It suggests selfishness and individual gain much more than cooperation and a common purpose.

Compare this statement with the following two, one made by a top executive in another U.S. Fortune 500 company, the other by a high-level Japanese manager in a large, Tokyo-based company. Both statements, like the preceding one, were made behind closed doors, not to impress outsiders.

> Our primary responsibility is to our customers. We owe them quality, safety, peace of mind, and good value at reasonable prices. In fact, we owe them our livlihood.
>
> Our job is to ensure that this responsbility is met. Company systems and operations must guarantee cooperation and attention to customer satisfaction. If we work together to accomplish this, other company and individual goals simply will fall into place.

> To attain goals consistent with our mission, company activities must concentrate on the effective monitoring of customers' needs. The customer comes first, for only he can ensure profitability and survival in a rapidly changing competitive world. There's no such answer as "That's not my job or responsbility" when it comes to customers. The customer is everybody's job and everybody's responsbility, and all of us must work together to guarantee his satisfaction.
>
> After taking care of customers, management activities then can focus on company obligations to shareholders, suppliers, the communities in which we operate, and the nation whose prosperity is inextricably linked to ours. We are only one piece in a big puzzle, and concerted, cooperative effort is needed to create a coherent picture.

The differences between the first statement and the latter two are striking indeed. One focuses attention on individual goals and gains, the others on the well-being of customers, owners, and even the nation. One suggests inertia, a continuation of style, incentives, and perqs, regardless of environmental changes and challenges. The latter two statements imply dynamism, adaptability, and the critical importance of externalities in keeping the company close to relevant stakeholders. The first statement implies an underlying inconsistency between individual needs and company goals, purpose, or mission, while the latter two suggest greater consonance between goals of individuals and those of the company in which they work.

Admitedly, I have an advantage; I know all three companies well and have seen their inherent differences firsthand. In the first case, the worst aspects of I-Force thinking abound. In the other two companies, in contrast, culture and operations reflect what I'm calling a We-Force, or systems of cooperation.

You may be wondering if these different cultures have any real importance. Who cares if differences in culture, values, and perspective exist if they don't make the slightest dent in earnings, return on owners' equity, or customer loyalty?

The critical point is that there *are* differences in performance. The first company, which had been successful for years, has steadily lost market share for a decade and has seen a major erosion in profitability. The latter two companies, in contrast, are performing quite well compared to other companies with a similar size, scope of operations, and product line. My work with the companies also has revealed significant differences in other measures of performance, including managerial turnover and customer loyalty. The first company is characterized by a dog-eat-dog climate and an overriding concern with internal politics that over the years have caused increased managerial turnover and a loss of customers. The latter companies have not suffered such detrimental outcomes. Differences in turnover and customer satisfaction contribute to the additional efficiency and effectiveness of the last two companies.

It is eminently clear to me that the ability of companies to create and sustain cooperation affects performance. The preceding three cases certainly do not explain all variance in performance across all companies. Still, my experience has shown that the We-Force has many beneficial consequences for companies and their managers. So let's consider the We-Force in greater detail.

What the We-Force Is

The We-Force represents coordinated, cooperative efforts and systems directed toward the accomplishment of agreed-upon, superordinate goals. The We-Force influences managerial motivation, company culture, decision processes, and important strategic and operating results. It defines a way of thinking about managing that departs significantly from other approaches to management and control. Let me share the seven prime tenets of the We-Force.

1. First and foremost, emphasis is on we, not I. The We-Force suggests that cooperation is often more effective than individual action in achieving complex outcomes. The We-Force organization fosters interdependence, cooperation, and a lateral perspective on information, decisions, and operations. As basic as it sounds, this picture of lateral communication, coordination, and cooperation is quite different from the traditional vertical view in many companies.

2. The We-Force relies on superordinate goals or a common company vision. Individual and departmental goals clearly are important but must be related to overarching common purposes. Cooperation is often thwarted by imperfect correlation between systemwide and individual or department goals.

Consider goals and rationality for a moment. Individuals are rational and pursue goals that provide benefit and personal reward. The sum of rational behaviors at the individual level, however, does not necessarily add up to rationality at a higher level of analysis. Individual rationality does not automatically mean company rationality. The We-Force focuses on superordinate company goals and the need to provide incentives for the common good, for individual incentives alone are not sufficient to achieve and sustain cooperation.

3. Sustainable cooperation depends on effective planning and change- management processes. In companies sustained by the We-Force, behavior is directed toward goals that help to define the cooperative system and give meaning to its activities. Goals must be shared, as stressed previously. It is also imperative that company decision processes allow for changes in goals. How superordinate goals are defined, refined, and changed affects cooperation and the sustainability of We-Force thinking.

4. The We-Force and its attendant coordination and cooperation must occur at all levels of organization and in all areas of responsibility. No level, function, or responsibility should be excluded from the processes that foster cooperation and coordination.

5. High levels of interdependence require communication of useful information. Organizational structure, incentives, and control systems must foster the sharing of information and speed of decision making vital to the We-Force.

6. Commitment to The We-Force depends on its effectiveness in achieving agreed-upon goals and in satisfying individual needs. Cooperative efforts must work. Whether talking about teamwork on strategic goals or short-term operating objectives, cooperation must add something of value. If beneficial results are lacking, the cooperative effort will disband and die.

But while the We-Force indicates coordinated, cooperative effort and superordinate goals, it does not negate or contradict the I-Force. Individuals must want to cooperate. Some correlation between individual and collaborative goals is absolutely critical. While individual and company goals occasionally may conflict, they more than occasionally must be in agreement. To survive, the We-Force must create something of value for the company and for the individuals who choose to cooperate. The We-Force, then, suggests a win-win situation, both for the company and the individuals involved in the cooperative effort.

7. Finally, the We-Force creates more effective managers. Emphasis on cooperation, coordination, and results breeds managers uniquely capable of managing under conditions of rapid change, uncertainty, and stress. Hypercompetition in many industries is forcing companies to respond more quickly and decisively than ever before to market shifts and competors' strategies. The We-Force emphasis on cooperation, lateral coordination, and effective incentives lends itself nicely to quick company adaptation and managers' ability to cope with uncertainty and change.

These are some of the aspects of the We-Force. They direct attention to superordinate goals, lateral communication, and productive harnessing of individual motivations. Although the We-Force creates behaviors, perceptions, and decisions that are different from those traditionally held in many U.S. companies, this new way of thinking has positive implications for individuals and their organizations.

This is not to say that this management style will be quickly embraced by all managers. Aspects of the We-Force methodology may trouble people accustomed to individual-driven management styles and systems. Nonetheless, global competition and rapidly changing market conditions demand new managerial capabilities, the very skills the We-Force engenders.

The concept of a We-Force as coordinated, cooperative effort is straightforward. The actual steps involved in creating and sustaining cooperation and teamwork, however, are not always simple. In fact, they can be quite challenging.

In my experience, the notions of cooperation and superordinate goals occasionally can foster tension between individuals and the organization. The latter, by definition, controls the discretion, actions, and choices of the former in many ways. If individuals resist, achieving cooperation can be difficult, if not impossible.

The cooperative system defined by the We-Force must be adaptive. The needs and motives of individuals change over time, as do organizational needs and goals. Maintaining or sustaining cooperation, then, demands flexibility, trust, risk taking, and a willingness to experiment and change—tasks that, in themselves, are challenging.

How, then, does one achieve the We-Force in an organization? What are the critical steps, decisions, or goals to be concerned about? What must be done, and in what logical order, to create and sustain cooperative efforts? The next chapter begins to answer these central questions.

4

The We-Force:
Start with Good Planning

Setting the stage for cooperation /
Anticipating problems that kill cooperation /
An ounce of prevention

The first step in creating and sustaining cooperation is good planning. What is "good" planning? As A. A. Milne tells us through the mouth of Christopher Robin in his classic *Winnie the Pooh*:

> Organizing is what you do before you do something, so that when you do it, it's not all mixed up.

Christopher Robin's definition of organizing also serves for planning. Planning anticipates. It prevents mistakes and surprises.

Most managers know a great deal about the content of plans. The content of corporate strategy, for example, includes financial brokerage, portfolio assessment, and decisions on what businesses the company should be in. The content of business-level strategies is focused on industry forces and how to position a company's products or services in a competitive environment. An action plan includes short-term measures of performance and the tactics employed to attain them.

I am not interested here in the content of planning. Most managers I've worked with can address planning content comfortably. They understand the logic of planning and its importance. They can perform the mechanical steps of planning, including industry and competitor analysis and creation of portfolio models to guide diversification and growth strategies.

Where many managers are weak, however, is in two planning-related areas. The first is inattention to critical processes that affect cooperation and the commitment to joint ventures. Included here are generating agreement on planning priorities, analyzing interdependence or needed areas of cooperation, ensuring consistency across units involved in planning, and creating a vision to unify diverse planning efforts.

The second area in which managers are deficient is preparation for the implementation of plans. Clarification of roles and responsibilities in the cooperative venture is a vital but often overlooked aspect of sound planning. Similarly, managers don't make the effort to define and track the *measurable results* of cooperation. If the outcomes of a joint effort cannot be specified nor its benefits shown clearly, commitment to cooperation will be low or nonexistent.

This chapter considers these overlooked aspects of planning. As I will show, good planning is a critical first step in creating a We-Force and the benefits it implies.

Creating the Vision

The first important aspect of good planning is to create a vision for the company or to reflect and reinforce the existing vision. A clear vision or sense of mission has extremely valuable instrumental and psychological benefits for a company. It helps in three main areas.

Providing a direction. Defining the business in terms of core products, services, or technologies indicates strategic intent. This vision helps immensely when the business confronts issues of growth or diversification by providing parameters to guide such decisions.

Setting priorities. Strategic and operating plans that most closely reflect the company vision must have priority for resources and action. These priorities guide decision making and help justify unpopular courses of action—for example, recalling tainted products at great expense or passing up quick profits in favor of long-term strategic growth.

Generating commitment. A commonly accepted mission or credo generates commitment and identification with important company goals and activities. It provides a bond or thread of consistency that can have positive psychological or instrumental outcomes—for example, reduced turnover.

Cooperation is eminently easier and more likely to occur when a common vision or credo drives managerial action. Commonly held beliefs, values, and perceptions of the business are instrumental in creating a We-Force and supporting its critical components, such as communication, participation, and delegation.

Participation: Getting the Right People Involved

We all know about the role and power of participation. Social psychologists, students of the Japanese experience, and numerous others have extolled its virtues. In fact, participation is a vital aspect of good planning.

Participation is central to the ownership and buy-in so desperately needed in cooperative systems. Participation is positively related to psychological identification, which boosts commitment to goals and the efforts to attain them.

Ownership and buy-in cannot occur under conditions of uncertainty or confusion. They require clear knowledge of the strategies or action plans that are being formulated. Participation reduces uncertainty by getting people with the requisite knowledge, skills, or competencies to help define the plan. Once they've helped to create the plan, they usually support its aims and methods.

To encourage participation, managers must delegate responsibilities and endow others below them with the rights of decision making. This strategy confirms that others in the company have instrumental value in planning and can positively affect participants' perceptions of self-worth and confidence.

Creating participation does not mean abdication. Participation carries important responsibilities and suggests a two-way, not a one-way, avenue of communication. Individuals who are empowered to do something are accountable for their actions and decisions. Similarly, those who delegate and empower others still share responsibility for the results of cooperative efforts. Participation requires a climate in which managers are expected to perform in ways that benefit the company and adhere to its vision.[1]

Participation, in brief, means active involvement and responsibility, which affect buy-in, commitment, and ownership. Caste systems break down because of participation in decisions, and the line between planners and doers disappears. Selection of participants must be based on the task at hand and the skills needed, not on individuals' level in the organization, politics, or invalid assumptions and superstitions (e.g., "lower levels don't really want to be involved in planning"). Participation leads to cooperation across levels and departments.

The Importance of Creating Agreement

Participative planning has an important corollary: it creates agreement within a company, especially among top-level decision makers. This agreement includes goals, strategies, tactics, the need for change, and other critical aspects of the plan. Without agreement, individuals from different functions, with different needs, bosses, technologies, and perceptions, would find no reason to cooperate.

Agreement can even affect industry structure by connecting or binding people from different companies. In Japan, for example, auto manufacturers deal with suppliers without the suspicion, distrust, and distance that, for years, have marked the U.S. industry. Rather, Japanese companies deal only with first-tier suppliers who, in turn, must coordinate efforts with second-tier suppliers, who work with third-tier suppliers. This system facilitates the sharing of information and technology.

Why does this system work? Because cooperation is the guiding principle, not competition. And cooperation is possible because of agreed-upon superordinate goals. These goals include survival in an increasingly competitive industry and desire for a long-term, stable relationship that can become a competitive advantage. A common goal also exists because all parties know that a single failure—for example, no parts available from a just-in-time inventory system—can seriously injure everyone. Agreement on superordinate goals is critical; it makes managers feel that they're in the same boat, pulling in the same direction.

Another reason to try to generate agreement is that the attempt may be profitable to a company. My research shows that top managers' agreement in defining their company's competitive strengths and weaknesses is positively related to profitability. The greater the agreement, the higher the return on assets, according to my study of eighty-eight companies in four different industries. Even when managers agree that something is wrong—for example, that a weakness or potential competitive disadvantage exists—agreement is still positively related to performance. A manager explains:

> If we all agree that our marketing group is weak, much weaker than that of our biggest competitors, we can do something about it. We can seek outside help. We can compensate for the weakness by doing other things.
>
> What's the worst thing that can happen? Having the weakest marketing group in the universe in some "objective" sense, but not having agreement on this critical fact. Without agreement, nothing changes, nothing will compensate for the weakness or problem. We'll go down the toilet and not even know or agree on why it's happening.

Agreement leads to consistency of purpose and focus, and it allows management to deal with important issues related to strategy, competition, core competence, and profitability. Achieving measurable results like increases in profitability reinforces the value of agreement and cooperative efforts. In contrast, widespread disagreement can only be divisive and disruptive, detracting significantly from meeting the organization's goals.

By now, I'm sure, you have certain questions as a result of reading this chapter. These probably resemble questions I've faced about participation, agreement, and cooperation from others in the past: How do mangers create agreement? What processes can stimulate involvement and generate commitment to goals? How do mangers identify key issues and superordinate goals? How does one get buy-in and widespread commitment to plans and actions?

There are group processes for identifying issues and generating agreement. One of the best is a nominal-group technique, although any well-run group process can achieve positive results.

The nominal-group technique has a number of simple steps for generating issues, setting priorities, and reaching consensus within the group. The steps in this simple but powerful process are summarized briefly in an appendix to this chapter.

Focus on Implementation

The most important part of planning is getting ready for doing. Without the doing part, planning is useless. If we don't know who's to do what, with what resources, and in what time frame, then planning is just a pie-in-the-sky game.

What this manager was telling me is that good planning focuses not only on formulating goals and strategies but, more importantly, on their implementation. It is imperative that planning not only answer the question of what should be done, but how, when, and by whom. Paying attention to implementation early in the planning process fosters cooperative efforts. It identifies key players and their responsibilities and also identifies areas of cooperation and joint decision making that might fall through the cracks at a later time.

I have been involved in planning processes in many companies where managers enjoyed creating the plan. Conceptualizing various issues, problems, and scenarios of action was truly enjoyable. Creative juices flowed as assumptions were tested and different competitive strategies and tactics were evaluated.

Cooperation was evident during the formulation of the plan. Working together seemed easy and natural as managers got into the hunt and offered their thoughts and proposals. The planning process obviously was a challenging and enjoyable sport to the players involved in a game of conceptualizing and creating.

The problem was that the formulating stage was the fun part. With the plan nearing its final form, the planners looked for other challenging and enjoyable tasks. As one manager expressed it when asked about implementation: "Hey, we've done our part. Carrying out the plan is somebody else's business. We've got lots of people around here who enjoy the work involved with execution and making things happen."

In essence, somebody else, somewhere out there in the company, is responsible for implementation. Someone else in the view of the planners, faces the more routine and less enjoyable task of executing the plan. In many cases, the implementors are not identified and the necessary tasks never fleshed out. Areas of joint or cooperative effort are assumed, but never clearly delineated. Assignments are not made because the creators of the plan presume that someone else would join forces and somehow make things happen.

In truth, things usually don't just happen. Lack of attention to implementation almost always guarantees problems and poor results. By assuming that doing is someone else's job or that results somehow will take care of themselves, planners create conditions ripe for inaction and little cooperation. As an executive in charge of the strategic planning process for an SBU of a large corporation put it:

> We learned the hard way that simply handing off the ball did not guarantee positive results. We once thought that the logic and attractiveness of a plan were sufficient to make others follow willingly and do the right things. That's not the case, however, not by a long shot. Planning doesn't end with formulation of the plan. What's needed to achieve the vision and make the plan work is a lot of time and effort devoted to the next steps. Implementation is a vital part of planning, especially who does what next, with whom, and in what time frame to achieve what results. Planning and doing are not separate and distinct, but part of the same overall process.

Several specific implementation issues arise with good planning.

Authority, responsibility, and interdependence. Who is responsible for what and who must work with whom for the desired results? This is such a vital topic that I return to it in greater detail in chapter 5.

Appropriate organizational structure. Good planning determines whether the current organizational structure is consistent with company strategic and operating plans. An emphasis on diversification into unrelated markets demands a different structure than adding additional products in the same market. Simarly, organizational structures for global competition include autonomous product divisions worldwide, use of an international indivision, or creation of a complex global matrix. Because each structure has its strengths and shortcomings, the choice of structure must follow logically from the global strategy being pursued[2]. Good planning must recognize this fact, early in the process.

Adequate coordination mechanisms. A scheme for coordination or integration should be part of the planning process. The methods or forms of coordination depend on the type and complexity of interdependence created by planning. Anticipating coordination—for example, integrating roles, cross-functional teams, even matrix-type structures—is part of sound planning and preparation for action and results.

Incentive and controls. Planning for one result but rewarding quite another clearly is inconsistent with company goals. Yet incentive and control systems often have this debilitating result. Good planning identifies such implementation inconsistencies and corrects them.

Planning both the goals and the processes to achieve them gets the job done, eliminates duplication of effort, and facilitates cooperation.

Be Consistent

How often have you seen individuals and groups doing things that are inconsistent with the goals or activities of others within the same company? How often have you observed managers working at cross-purposes?

One department's quest for low-cost production hurts another's strategy of high-quality products or impeccable customer service. Or a division in a vertically integrated company makes its profits by overcharging end-user divisions in the same company. Or one profit center (e.g., a distributor or retailer) refuses to carry certain low-margin products from another profit center (e.g., a product division), despite the products' importance for volume and overall company efficiency.

As obvious as these problems seem to be, detecting inconsistencies is often difficult. One reason for this difficulty is that each individual or unit is acting rationally, pursuing objectives that appear beneficial to the company. Each individual and unit, when considered separately, apparently is doing the right things, making sound business decisions.

These inconsistencies can hurt the company. Even if unintended, areas of conflict can be harmful to cooperation and company performance and, therefore, must be identified and eliminated. According to the executive in charge of SBU planning who was cited previously, this job begins with good planning:

> The task of every manager involved in planning is to take one step backward and look up, down, and sideways. To reduce the possibility of one unit's meat becoming another's poison, our planning process now forces managers to analyze and weigh the intended and possible unintended consequences of their actions on other units in the company. Part of a planning worksheet is actually titled "Negative Consequences," where managers list the potential downside results of a plan for other parts of the company. This analysis is not optional; every unit manager must do it to ensure that we're not hurting each other in our individual attempts to look good.

Think Minutes, Days . . . , and Decades

The same emphasis on consistency arises when considering the integration of plans over time. Managers constantly must be aware of the relationship between short-term and long-term performance. Tactical plans and activities must contribute to strategic, longer-term plans and objectives. At minimum, the short term must not work to the detriment of the long term.

I once heard a disciple of Dr. Edward Deming say that companies need people who "manage by the hour" and some who "manage by the decade." I would add that more than ever companies need both viewpoints in the same managers. Companies need people who, while managing by the hour, day, or quarter, are constantly aware of their responsibilities for the decade. One such manager balances the present and the future with a few simple questions.

> Whenever I, as a manager, make an important decision, I *always*, repeat, *always*, ask myself the same simple questions: "What if I owned this business? What if this company belonged to me and my family? What effects would my decision today have on me and my family five or ten years down the road?"
>
> These questions work for me. Don't give me any fancy talk about long run and short run, whatever they are. I look at things in a simple way. If I were the owner of the company, would I still be happy with myself and my decisions when my son or daughter is in charge?

A goal of good planning, then, is to question and look for possible inconsistencies over time. Good planning must focus on the long and short term simultaneously. It is important that the conflicts and inconsistencies potentially injurious to cooperation and common goals be identified early and exorcised from a company. Good planning helps in this regard.

First, Do No Harm

> Whatever else a hospital is or does, it should never cause illness. Likewise, whatever else managers do, they should not cause problems for a company.

Care must be taken to ensure that planning does not create problems for the company, as the executive quoted above warns. You can use some planning guidelines to help prevent the creation of problems and a backlash against cooperation.

Never use all-or-nothing objectives. Planning fosters a win-lose mentality if it sets up all-or nothing objectives. "Make 100 percent of your objective and you're OK, maybe even a hero. Make 99 percent and you're a bum, a loser. Even if [a competitor] does worse than you, you're still tainted or tarnished because you didn't make it. Know what the difference is around here between 100 percent and 99 percent? It's really 100 percent, not a lousy 1 percent!"

If negative sanctions are attached to "not making it," a fear of failure creates tension and eliminates risk taking. Everything is focused on meeting individual objectives, certainly not helping others make theirs. When contributing to the common good clearly is less important than achieving individual milestones, cooperation suffers.

Avoid excessive competition. Planning can create excessive competition for scarce resources. In extreme cases, a dog-eat-dog mentality can kill cooperation.

Planning under high-levels of competition can lead to low-balling, especially when all-or-nothing objectives exist. Low-balling fascillitates making all-or-nothing objectives and avoiding becoming a bum. It helps people appear to make the grade and to look better than others. This game of low-balling and one-upmanship can create tensions and make cooperation unlikely, at best. At worst, it can lead to open warfare or sabotage, which clearly destroys joint efforts.

Don't create stereotypes. In some cases, planning can lead to destructive stereotyping. Labeling a particular product line or division a "dog" in the planning process causes others to begin to treat it as such. Resources for the dog get cut and its performance suffers, leading to additional cuts down the road. Performance suffers further, and before long someone will remark: "See, I told you that division was a dog!" In some cases, the dog really may be a loser; in others, the label creates a self-fulfilling prophesy: who wants to set up cooperative ventures or associate with a dog? Working closely with a dog may be hazardous to one's health, as association breeds identification and further stereotyping. Even stars can create resentment, as they are seen as the chosen, gobbling up scarce resources disproportionately. This perception, of course, also can affect cooperation.

Focus on Measurable Results

One significant factor in the failure of cooperation is methodological: the inability to measure cooperation and its outcomes. Good planning must develop objectives that are measurable and meaningful. If cooperation is looked down upon as a warm and fuzzy process and the outcomes and utility of cooperative effort cannot be gauged and rewarded, the motivation to pursue joint decision making and shared ventures will wane and disappear.

The problem is twofold: (a) as stressed previously, managerial motivations reflect an I-Force, an emphasis on individual achievement, measurement, and reward; and (b) because measuring the results of cooperation and shared effort is often seen as difficult, managers are dissuaded from the effort. In fact, the two problems are interdependent. If measurability is achieved and managers see the fruits of cooperative behavior, the chances that they will be motivated by We-Force thinking increase dramatically.

To ensure the measurability of cooperation and its results, a number of steps, actions, or foci are recommended.

Separate Process and Outcome

Many companies emphasize process when describing a cooperative effort. People talk about social interaction, feeling good, or how group process leads to job satisfaction. Or emphasis is put on the time and effort expended.

> We literally lived together for two weeks preparing this proposal. The RFP [Request for Proposal] made many demands, some of which were really ambiguous. We had to iron things out and decide what we were going to emphasize. There was a lot of give and take, argument, and compromise. But you know what? We got the damn thing done and it really felt good. Somehow we didn't mind all the work and overtime when we saw the finished product.

Feeling good about the cooperative effort certainly is worthwhile and important. What the manager's quote here doesn't reveal, however, is that the job was not won. The proposal development felt good, but it was ineffective. In fact, the win rate for this company was miserable and the costs per win were extremely high.

Proposal writing or preparation was a crisis activity that generated excitement and a large number of proposals, but the outcomes were poor and costly, as few proposals were accepted by customers.

Focus on Outcomes

It is imperative, then, to emphasize the results of cooperation. Focusing on outcomes in the planning process forces managers to define and operationlize them or, at minimum, the proxy measures that suggest the desired outcomes.

In the proposal-writing case, emphasis was shifted to results. The focus was on win rate, costs, and profits generated through the proposal-writing activity. The criteria of effective proposals were researched and actively built into future proposal development and measurements of success.

One way we did this was to talk to customers and seek their criteria for judging the worth of cooperation and the characteristics of sound proposals. Procedures then were developed to ensure that proposal writing focused on the market-based criteria. This, in turn, helped the company create standards to determine the composition of the proposal-writing group—that is, who should be part of the cooperative process.

"Best practices" to achieve consistent proposal development and desired outcomes were also instituted within the company to avoid reinventing the wheel each time they responded to customers' RFPs. Both processes and outcomes were studied to reduce costs, eliminate duplications of effort, and increase the attractiveness of the company's proposals to its market. These efforts to define proposal-writing procedures and objectives have paid off handsomely, for the emphasis on outcomes has improved the company's win rate while reducing costs.

Other ideas often mentioned when seeking cooperation and its results likewise need operationalization and effective measures. Consider the example of *synergy,* an often espoused goal of cooperation. Synergy sounds good, and managers nod approvingly when it is featured as a desired outcome of joint effort. But how does one measure synergy? By focusing on outcomes and defining the effects of synergistic collaboration. Such outcomes and effects might include the following areas.

Economies of scale or scope. Working together, producing a greater volume of work, developing repetitive tasks, and increasing individual productivity through learning and experience can generate measurable economies or efficiencies that reflect synergy. Variable costs per unit, for instance, decrease as a result of synergy. This is true in a manufacturing firm where variable costs include the materials used or in a government agency where variable costs include overtime pay or consultants' fees.

New product or service development and its consequences. Creative teams, pushing the envelopes of technology and knowledge, develop heady and enjoyable climates in which to work. But how can their success be measured? One answer, reflecting synergy, is the number of new products or services developed over a given period of time and the logical consequences for the company in terms of market share, revenues, patents won, or new customers gained. Customers' satisfaction with the teams' innovations and cooperative efforts between company and customer representatives also can provide a measure of synergistic results.

Effects on turnover. Synergy supposedly feels good. Its balance of autonomy and social interaction within a setting of interdependence and common goals should produce a positive work environment that is desired by managers. It is logical, then, to hypothesize and test for the impact of this beneficial climate on costly outcomes, such as turnover. It isn't always easy to isolate the impact of synergy versus other factors on outcomes like turnover, but identifying such consequences of synergy is possible and worthy of managerial attention.

Another often-espoused outcome of cooperation is a focus on the *common* good, a superordinate purpose or mission in a company that overrides purely individual goals. The critical task here is to separate and measure individual and collective outcomes.

Individual versus collective outcomes. Individual rationality is no guarantee of collective rationality, as emphasized previously. Two functional managers may pursue low-cost production or a cost leadership position, on one hand, and product differentiation via customer service and product customization, on the other. Each functional manager is focusing logically and unerringly on individual goals that appear to be eminently rational and utilitarian—for example, efficiency, reduced variable cost per unit, customer satisfaction, and higher margins of product differentiation. But summing the two performances may result in poor collective performance if their functional goals are incompatible—for example, when low-cost approaches injure the basis of product differentiation.

The need, then, is to define collective outcomes. The focus should be on company profits rather than on individual or subunit profits; overall customer satisfaction or market share changes that result from the integration of different functions or company units; and planning processes that differentiate performance measures across company levels—corporate, business, functional—and then eliminate the conflicts and inconsistencies that are found among them. Return on investment objectives can be in conflict and create dysfunctional behavior when the return is measured on different investment bases—for example, SBU versus corporate—and performing well on one criterion hurts performance against the other.

Analyze Tasks for Cause and Effect Relationships

Earlier discussions of the measurable outcomes of cooperation assumed that cause and effect will be analyzed, but this step is important enough to emphasize separately. It is essential to evaluate tasks and build models of cause and effect to explain the results of cooperation.

Some tasks can be analyzed more easily than others, depending on their outcomes, technologies, and problem-solving processes. For example, it is easier to analyze and explain why paint doesn't adhere to metal in a manufacturing and product-finishing process than it is to explain why discharged, supposedly cured mental patients occasionally relapse and have to return to an institution. The material being worked on or with clearly has different characteristics, such as malleability, complexity, and variability. Paint and metal obviously are different from complex human beings in many ways. Still, the process of explaining cause and effect is similar. It involves (a) determining the key causal factors, variables, or forces; (b) building alternative cause-and-effect models to explain outcomes; and (c) reaching agreement on what measures of outcome will be used.

The difficulty of building and testing models of cause and effect will vary. With paint's adherence to metal, the analysis is relatively easy, as engineers work through the process of manufacturing, assembly, and painting armed with their knowledge of the physical and engineering sciences and of the conditions under which paint will or will not stick. Psychiatrists face a more daunting task in explaining the behavior of their patient. Still, they must evaluate the effects of different types of therapy, the impact of different drugs, and the weight of personal characteristics like age when explaining relapse rates. The physicians may even need to set up controlled experiments to explain why group or cooperative setting (for example, group psychotherapy) is better than other forms of treatment, but a focus on outcomes often demands such attention and effort.

In both cases, then, the desired results include a better understanding of cause and effect, of the technologies employed (painting or group psychotherapy), and of the outcome of individual or cooperative effort. Specific changes follow logically from this analysis. These might include altering the temperature at which paint is applied or revising the definition of "cure" and the requirements for discharge from the psychiatric hospital. The crucial point is that the changes must be justified and explained by an analysis of the means and a focus on outcomes or results.

Seek Outside Help

In the planning process, it is often wise to cooperate with outsiders on establishing and measuring internal cooperative objectives.

Take the example of vertical integration, in which an upstream unit or SBU is charged with delivering a product or service to a downstream unit or SBU. Assume that managers in the upstream unit wish to work together to increase output to their internal customer. Assume, too, that they wish to improve the quality of their work for the customer but that they also are under intense pressure to reduce costs. Their task, then, is to redefine results in ways that improve quality and customer satisfaction while simultaneously reducing the costs associated with the effort.

The best way the upstream unit could redefine its output and measures of cooperative effort, consistent with the constraints noted, would be to ask for help from the downstream customer.

The supplier can ask the user unit a number of questions, real or hypothetical, to uncover critical measures of output and cooperative effort. These would include, but are not limited to:

- How do you judge or measure our performance? On what criteria?
- If, hypothetically, we did a good job one week and a very poor one the next, how could you tell? Based on what indicators or measurable parameters?
- What are the discernible differences between inadequate and adequate quality in the products you receive? How do you measure the differences?
- How can we change our products or services to improve quality? Do you have any ideas about lowering costs without hurting product performance or quality?

Directing questions like these to customers is especially important in service businesses or staff functions, such as MIS or Human Resources. I've often heard service people or functional support staff personnel complaining about how to describe and measure their performance.

> It's difficult to measure what we do. Unlike manufacturing, we don't deal with parts, components, or products, but with support activities. We're different. You can't measure our performance or easily calculate what we do.

The problem here is obvious and recurring. Someone inevitably tries to analyze the support function's contribution to the company or customer.

> If we can't measure what they do, how can we evaluate their performance or the requests for additional resources? If we can't define their contributions, why do we need them in the first place?

By asking customers about services, support activities, and measures of performance, service organizations and support functions can learn a great deal about how others measure and judge the quality of their outputs. This can only help the planning process and the setting of meaningful goals.

Seeking help from customers or other functions or groups, both within the company and outside it, can help immensely when defining the measures and results of cooperation. The success of cooperation depends on its specification and measurement, as well as on its results or outcomes. It is important to get as much assistance as possible on this vital aspect of the planning and objective-setting process.

Identifying Interdependence

There is yet one more way in which good planning affects coordination and cooperation, and it is as vital as all the points discussed previously. Planning must identify points of interdependence—areas where people must cooperate and work together.

Interdependence lies at the heart of cooperative systems. The arena within which coordination, communication, and joint decision making exist and critically affect performance must be defined during planning. Chapter 5 treats planning, interdependence, and cooperation in greater detail.

Appendix: The Nominal-Group Technique

The nominal-group technique can help generate agreement. It can be described as an eight-step process.

Step 1: Individuals work alone on a problem or issue—for example, identifying the biggest competitive challenges facing the company over the next five years. Ideally, the problem has been defined or presented for consideration well before a meeting. Participants are urged to work alone to ensure fresh, individual ideas and to avoid early group-think. The important thing is for participants to create a list of items independently, free from social pressure and with sufficient time, so they will not be forced into premature conclusions or closure on the issues.

Step 2: A group meeting is held to generate a list of all the issues. One by one, around the table, individuals provide one of the issues from their list to a facilitator. Criticism and commentary are ruled out. Questions of clarification are permitted. The listing proceeds continuously, one person and one item at a time, until all the participants report that they have nothing else to list. The facilitator of the meeting records the points on a flip-chart.

Step 3: An open group discussion of all the issues listed is next. Individuals criticize the items and perhaps eliminate some from the list. They look for redundancies and ways of categorizing the items logically. Priorities are discussed, and ways of determining the relative importance of items or groups of items are considered. The facilitator can bring out normally reticent or quiet people by asking them to elucidate or explain the thinking behind their points.

Step 4: Individuals are separated (to avoid social pressure, peeking at a neighbor's listing, etc.) and asked to vote on the items. For example, they might be asked to choose the five most important items from the entire list of twenty-five issues. Sufficient time is provided so that participants don't have to rush. Points are assigned, with five points given to the most important item, four points to the next most important, three points, and so on.

Step 5: Votes are tabulated and total points are assigned to each item. A subset of the original items is chosen, based upon the points received. The size of the subset depends upon point distribution and the group's ad-hoc decision on a cut-off point. For example, out of twenty-five items, five to eight might be chosen for further discussion. The group then repeats step 3, discussing and evaluating the subset of items, with an added emphasis on relative importance and priorities.

Step 6: Repeat step 4, but now vote for a smaller number of items. For example, vote for the top three items, assigning a score of three to the most important, and so on.

Step 7: Tabulate the results. Focus on points of agreement. Confront any disagreements on the most critical strategic issues facing the company. Generate visible agreement on and commitment to the chosen issues among the group members. This can be done by identifying dissenting members and asking them, "Despite your lack of enthusiasm for the group's priorities, can we count on your [your function's] support?" "Although you disagree with our preferred actions or thrust, the rest of us depend heavily on your support or expertise. Because we are so interdependent, will you agree here, before all of us today, to provide that support or expertise?" It is critically important that dissenters make a visible commitment of some kind as a first step toward supporting behaviors later.

Step 8: Based upon the issued identified, decide which people will be responsible for developing an implementation plan or planning the next stages of action or discussion. This step is vital. Planning denotes action and problem-solving, and real solutions and actions must be identified as a natural outcome of the group process.

Step 9: Follow up the decisions made or the steps implemented. This action suggests that the outcomes of steps 1–8 are vital to company success. It also allows for change, fine-tuning, or adapting the plan over time. As a result of the follow-up, additional problems or opportunities could generate other meetings or nominal group activities.

The nine steps in this nominal-group process can enable managers to focus on any number of strategic and operating issues. It can be a powerful tool in generating agreement and commitment to a task. For further information on this technique, see note 3 at the back of the book.

5

Interdependence: Who Must Work with Whom? Why? How?

Interdependence: The basis of cooperation /
When is cooperation needed? /
How to manage interdependence effectively

Who's the busiest guy by far in this company? That's easy. It's "someone"! Someone is responsible for everything. Who'll take care of the coordination on a project? Don't worry, someone will. Will the project requirements be pulled together for customer examination? Of course! Where? Well, obviously, someone, somewhere must be responsible for that!

Managing interdependence is critical to successful cooperation. Interdependence defines who must work with whom. It assumes that people know who's responsible for what and, thus, can identify where teamwork is essential. Sad to say, things usually are not this clear and straightforward, as the manager's biting lament above indicates. People often have no idea who and where "someone" is.

Different kinds of cooperation are needed in a company. This chapter addresses how to manage interdependence effectively, including how to determine responsibility or accountability for critical tasks, how to use teams effectively, and how to determine the form of cooperation that is needed.

Types of Interdependence

To define interdependence, I'll begin with the types introduced years ago by J. D. Thompson, for they are still useful.[1]

Pooled Interdependence

The first type of interdependence is pooled, a very low level of interdependence. Consider the sales organization illustrated in figure 5.1. This configuration shows pooled interdependence. Each district sales manager works in a separate geographical location. The territory could be part of a state, country, or even the world, but each is relatively defined, self-contained, and independent. Each sales manager responds to the particular needs of his or her district. There is little need for active, ongoing communication or coordination across districts. This is a case in which, typically, the sales managers work alone together.

While they work separately—focusing vertically rather than laterally across districts, so to speak—the word "together" in the previous sentence suggests some interdependence. If, for example, the bonus of each manager is based, in part, on overall or corporate earnings as well as regional performance, interdependence is clear. One manager may perform outstandingly, but poor performance by the others obviously can detract from the high performer's rewards.

Even pooled interdependence suggests, then, that people in an organization in some ways are in the same boat. The term "organization" denotes communality of some kind, even if ongoing communication and coordination are not the norm.

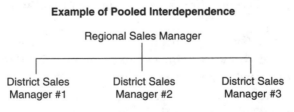

Example of Pooled Interdependence

Regional Sales Manager

District Sales Manager #1   District Sales Manager #2   District Sales Manager #3

Figure 5.1

Example of Sequential Interdependence

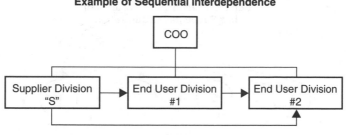

Figure 5.2

Sequential Interdependence

The next type is sequential interdependence, which is more complex than the pooled variety. Consider the simple case of vertical integration shown in figure 5.2. In this example, the flow of work or materials is sequential. Work flows from S, the supplier, to two end-user divisions. Semifinished goods also flow from end-user division 1 to division 2. The movement of product or service is unilateral or unidirectional.

Comparing sequential to pooled interdependence reveals that the cost of failure is higher in the former. In the pooled case, each district office looks and acts like the diagram in figure 5.3. As illustrated, each office does its own thing. A problem at D_1 does not directly and immediately affect D_2 or D_3. Routine communication and coordination across D_1, D_2, and D_3 are not vital to ongoing operations. Sequential interdependence is different, and can be represented by the illustration in figure 5.4. Problems at A not affect only A, they also affect B directly, and C and D directly and indirectly. Poor materials from the supplier division in the example have a direct, immediate impact on the end-user divisions.

**Communication and Coordination
in a Pooled Organization**

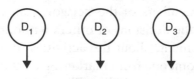

Figure 5.3

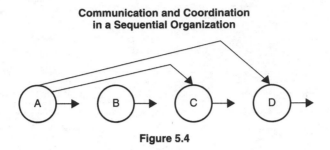

Figure 5.4

In addition, communication and coordination laterally, across A, B, C, and D, clearly are essential to ensuring smooth flows of work and success. Managers in all four locations have something at stake under sequential interdependence. The operation of the overall cooperative system defined by the sequential chain is vital to each individually. So, communication and coordination laterally affect both the overall system of vertical integration and the parts of that system at work.

The greater complexity of sequential interdependence demands that this form be managed differently than the pooled variety. Methods of coordination and control are different. These differences in method are spelled out later. First, however, let's consider a third type of interdependence.

Reciprocal Interdependence

Reciprocal interdependence is the most complex form and the most difficult to manage. Consider the representation in figure 5.5. In this case, every actor deals with everyone else. A (a person, department, etc.) both affects and is affected by, B, C, D, and E. What's more, one actor can change the rules or affect much of what is done by the others, at virtually any time.

Coordination and control under reciprocal interdependence are difficult, for many things are going on simultaneously. Planning is difficult, because members of the network can change their positions or even veto the decisions of others without warning.

Think, for a moment, about the activities of a new product development team. Someone from marketing contacts a potential customer and asks what she would like. The marketing manager brings

Example of Reciprocal Interdependence

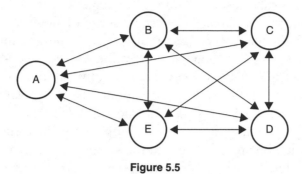

Figure 5.5

the information to engineering, where the product design must occur. Engineering's response is, "Sorry, there's no way we can design that." Marketing goes back to the customer and asks what else she would take. When the new request is brought to engineering, the response now is, "You must be kidding!"

By now the marketing manager is throwing up his hands in frustration. "What can you design?" he finally demands from engineering. But when he brings what's possible to the potential customer, she is not at all interested. Back to the drawing board. And so on—back and forth, give and take.

At last, marketing, engineering, and the customer agree on a viable product. They finally can bring the specifications and the product requirements to production. Much to their chagrin, however, the production guy says, "Sorry, there's no way in hell I can make something like this. With the pressure on me for volume and low-cost production, this product would kill me. Maybe next time."

Obviously, the production manager has affected engineering, marketing, and the customer. He has negated much of their effort. He is able to veto what others have spent a great deal of time pursuing. This type of case is not uncommon under reciprocal interdependence. All are equals in the decision process, and any player can affect all the others.

For a reciprocally interdependent system to work, it is imperative that cooperation be high. Cooperation, in turn, makes great demands on communication, coordination, and methods of reaching agreement. Clearly, reciprocal interdependence is difficult to manage. If mishandled, it can certainly create a mess.

Managing Interdependence and Cooperation Effectively

The next critical question is how to manage interdependence and foster cooperation. Table 5.1 presents some of these management methods. The table shows, first, that managing pooled interdependence is relatively easy. Standard operating procedures (SOPs) govern all of the independent individuals equally (all district managers report sales in the same way, all submit quarterly plans). When problems or unusual cases pop up, the role of hierarchy becomes important—resolving disputes, handling exceptions, and so on. People work alone together, but in the same or consistent ways.

Pooled interdependence does not generate the need for ongoing, active cooperation and coordination. The SOPs used for control and coordination are consistent for all units, but few, if any, deal with integration across units. Similarly, reliance on hierarchy stresses vertical communication, not lateral forms.

Sequential interdependence, as shown in table 5.1, raises the cost of sound management. Managing cooperation is more complex, and more time and resources must be devoted to the task. SOPs and hierarchy still play a role, but other more complex issues surface when focusing on cooperation in the value chain. Planning and scheduling are critical to smooth, predictable flows of work and materials. Poor planning or scheduling can lead to task interruptions and conflicts, which clearly detract from coordination, communication, and cooperation.

Managing transactions and lateral transitions of work from unit to unit is central to sequential interdependence. Tasks and activities within units are important, but so are the linkages between adjoining work groups. Transfer pricing in the vertical integration example, for instance, is vital to effective linkages. Inappropriate pricing affects not only work flow, but perceptions and cooperation as well.

Similarly, the quality of the products or services being transferred affects perceptions and the viability of cooperation. Consider the following comments made by managers in a vertically integrated company:

> I'm getting gouged price-wise by my own supplier, which happens to be a sister division in the same company. Nice, isn't it?

TABLE 5–1

Methods of Coordination and Control for Different Types of Interdependence and Levels of Cooperation

Type of Interdependence	Level of Cooperation Required	Methods of Achieving Coordination and Control
Pooled	Low	S.O.Ps/Hierarchy
Sequential	High	Coordination by plan
		Scheduling/just-in-time inventory controls
		"Transfer" activities—e.g. transfer pricing, terms to facilitate "passing of the baton"
		Feedback loops and Communication to different parts of value-added chain
		Appropriate incentives
Reciprocal	Very high	Coordination by "mutual adjustment"
		Face-to-face interaction, or managing by "living together"
		Removing administrative and geographical barriers
		Fostering communication processes of agreement, and trust
		Appropriate incentives

He sells all the good stuff outside, and sends me the rest, the junk. Why do I have to be stuck this way?

The state of cooperation between these divisions should be obvious. It is clear that perceptions as well as work flows under vertical integration depend heavily upon sound planning, communication, and coordination.

Some problems are specific to each part of the sequential chain, but other problems cut across the parts. Consider the case of a functional organization whose parts must be coordinated to achieve unity of effort. Assume that the marketing division loses a major customer. Whose problem is it? Under conditions of poor cooperation, the answer from a supplier or production function (early in the sequential chain) about marketing (later in the chain, closest to customers) might be:

> Hell, don't blame us. Losing a customer is marketing's problem. We only supply them. If they can't work with and satisfy customers, then they're screwed up, not us. Soon as something goes wrong, they look right away for a damn scapegoat.

This quote is from a manager in a company I once worked with. The prognosis for cooperation and problem solution obviously was not very good. Compare the preceding reaction to another in a company trying to follow the Deming methods for quality.

> The customer is upset, really ticked off. We've got to get the customer, marketing, engineering, and production together. We've got to get involved to find out what the customer wants and what the hell went wrong. Let's look at this as an opportunity for improvement and work on it fast. If we keep this up and don't change, all of us will be looking for a job.

In this case, the different units in the sequential chain were not treated as separate and independent. Customer satisfaction was seen as the result of integrated efforts across the units, not only the efforts of marketing, the unit closest to the customer. A cross-functional team was set up to work with the customer, and both the customer and company people defined improvement goals. Together they discussed and operationalized the methods and processes needed to test results and achieve the goals. Emphasis was on teamwork and the customer's needs, not on each function's covering its butt and finding others to blame for the negative results.

The example emphasizes the importance of cooperation, communication, feedback, and incentives under conditions of sequential interdependence. All of these issues become more complex in managing the third type of interdependence.

With reciprocal interdependence, coordination and control are extremely difficult to manage. Under this type, the other forms of interdependence also exist, so many of the previously identified problems are again important. But there are also new obstacles, as table 5.1 shows.

The need for cooperation is very high, as all of the members in the network affect and are affected by all of the other members. All have something at stake. Remember the new product development team discussed previously. One person under reciprocal interdependence can negate the work of others, even after significant amounts of time and effort have been expended.

Because of the impact of any one member, cooperation greatly relies on face-to-face interaction. Coordination and control are by "mutual adjustment" or, as a manager once expressed it to me, "managing by living together."

In the case of the new product development team, problem definition and solution ideally should be done together, with all team members participating simultaneously. All individuals should be "locked up together," with no one leaving until agreement is reached on critical aspects of the new product. Working alone together clearly is ruled out in this case.

But managing by mutual adjustment or living together is not always easy. Key team players involved in complex tasks might be spread out geographically or administratively. They might be all over the company, country, or world, in different functions or divisions, and even at different hierarchical levels. Getting them together and ensuring communication, agreement, and cooperation can be difficult.

Still, reciprocal interdependence demands that the attempt be made. Getting people together physically or linking them via telecommunications technologies is expensive, but necessary for effective coordination. Table 5.1 mentions some methods of achieving the requisite integration, and these are expanded upon in chapter 8. Many opportunities and problems facing companies create reciprocal interdependence. Managers, therefore, must tackle the issue head on and create the methods and incentives to foster the necessary interactions.

Identifying the type of interdependence, then, defines the level, and kind of cooperation necessary, as well as the management methods needed for coordination and control. Once the proper cooperative systems and methods are defined, additional attention can be paid to incentives and other factors that reinforce cooperation and sustain a We-Force over time. Only one more important point must be emphasized to complete our discussion of interdependence.

Responsibility and Accountability

In the preceding discussions of interdependence and cooperation was a basic but critical assumption: namely, that all responsibilities and accountabilities are clear. All individuals understand the interdependence and know what their roles or jobs are. Managers know with whom they must interact, and they are fully cognizant of others' tasks or duties. In short, the assumption is that the jobs, responsibilities, authority, and accountability of all interdependent actors are clear and well understood. Cooperation cannot occur if this understanding does not exist.

In reality, this clarity of roles is not always the case. The complexity of interdependence and cooperation often works against such understanding and clarity. Job-related responsibilities are not always clear and authority is not always unambiguous. Responsibility and accountability often are blurred when people from different functions or divisions come together, often from different hierarchical levels in the organization. This is especially true in simultaneous structures, like matrix organizations, where both lateral and hierarchical influences can easily cloud the responsibility and accountability picture.

Consider responsibility for a moment. On one hand, confusion results from multiple points of responsibility. Many managers share responsibility. As one manager in this situation once observed, when asked who was responsible for the quality of a particular product: "Around here, we're all responsible for quality. We all worry about it."

No problem; sounds good so far. But what happens when there is no central, integrating source of responsibility and authority? When those responsible for quality are found in different functions or have different perceptions or measures of quality? *When everyone is responsible, then no one is responsible.*

This situation isn't as far-fetched as it may sound. In fact, it is fairly common, especially in organizations trying to adapt to widespread or rapid change. Roles and responsibilities transform quickly as managers try to cope with change. When many individuals and skills are brought to bear on a problem or opportunity, the overarching authority or responsibility often becomes muddled over time. Hence, everyone's responsible; everyone must worry about the problem or opportunity. Yet the problem is never solved when everyone is responsible for it.

A related difficulty is when no one really feels responsible or accountable for an issue, goal, or task at hand. In the previous example, everyone felt responsible to some degree, but in this opposite case, no individual feels responsible or authorized to address a problem. Each individual believes that someone else, somewhere, is responsible or accountable. Consider something fairly basic, such as product line profitability.

Picture in your mind an organization with product managers at lower hierarchical levels, within functions (see figure 5.6). Each product line manager is responsible for a product within one department, such as manufacturing, engineering, or marketing. Each feels that profit responsibility exists for the entire line, across departments. But where? Product managers are shocked to learn that, at worst, no one is directly accountable. At best, the top person— the CEO—is accountable, ultimately, but certainly not in an operational sense. Add many other product lines and the confusion regarding product line profitability only increases.

It is also clear from figure 5.6 that coordination across functions is vital to the successful design, development, manufacture, and marketing of a product line. But who is responsible for coordination? Each product line manager performs functionally related tasks, but responsibility for overall integration certainly is not clear

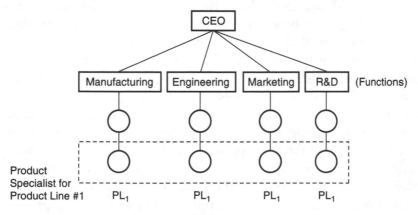

A Case of Unclear Responsibilities for a Product Line

Figure 5.6

from the figure. The assumption is that someone will initiate action and focus on the task of coordination across functions. But, again, hoping for or assuming something and getting it done are quite different things. Coordination needs are very likely to fall through the cracks.

Identifying interdependence is the cornerstone, the first key step in forming and creating cooperation. So, what can be done when people don't know who is interdependent with whom or who is responsible for what? When rapid change muddles the overall picture of authority?

Responsibility Plotting and Role Negotiation

One answer is responsibility plotting and role negotiation. These processes can help identify interdependence and areas in which cooperation is vital to successful performance. Several steps are involved in the process.[2]

The first step is to identify issues or tasks that are important to the company, but about which there might be confusion regarding interdependence, responsibility, and accountability. The second step is to construct a responsibility matrix for each issue or task (see table 5.2). Major activities or decisions relating to the task are shown on one axis, and important roles or positions are shown on the other.

The third step is to define different types or degrees of responsibility. The types must be relevant but simple and few enough to ensure manageability. Examples of the types or degrees of responsibility or authority might include: R, for the role ultimately *responsible* for an activity or decision; the requisite authority is there to make decisions. C, for the role of those who must be *consulted* prior to making a decision and who must be part of coordination plans. I, for the role of those who must be *informed* after a decision. ?, when you don't know whether this role is involved or what the extent of its involvement should be. The fourth step is to fill out the chart by assigning the appropriate responsibility codes to the major activities or decisions. In table 5.2, for example, the vice-presidents of manufacturing and marketing have responsibility and final authority over instituting a just-in-time system and revising product line prices, respectively.

TABLE 5-2

A Responsibility Matrix

Issue or Task: To improve overall quality and profitability of a Product Line.

Major Activities or Decisions	V.P. Manufacturing	V.P. Engineering	V.P. Finance	V.P. Marketing	Product Line Specialists
			Roles		
1. Institute just-in-time inventory system	R		C		C, I, ?
2. Ensure continuous process improvement	R	R	C	R	R
3. Determine customer requirements/definition of quality	R	R	C	R	R
4. Determine current profit margins and devise plan to increase profitability	?	?	?	?	?
5. Revise product line prices			C	R	
6. Reduce product costs			C		

R This role is ultimately *responsible* for an activity or decision; the requisite authority is there to make decisions.
C This role is *consulted* prior to making a decision, and must be part of *coordination* plans.
I This role is *informed* after a decision.
? Don't know if this role is involved or what should be the extent of its involvement.

The matrix can be filled out privately (individually) or publicly (in a group). It is extremely useful to do both. When charts done privately by individuals are compared and discussed later in an open, public forum, gross differences in perceptions of responsibility and authority often are revealed. Ironing out the differences clearly can do much to clarify the situation and determine where interdependence exists. Such role analysis and clarification often are vital to determining where cooperation is necessary. Such analysis also helps to identify the type or extent of cooperation needed to ensure successful performance.

The fifth and final step is the adjustment of roles and the redefinition of responsibility and authority consistent with the comparisons and analyses of the previous steps. Table 5.2 shows, for example, that as a result of a hypothetical analysis everyone is responsible for activities 2 and 3. No one knows who's responsible for activity number 4. The role of the product specialist exhibits confusion on activity number 1. Why is the vice-president of finance consulted on almost everything? Is this step necessary in a task-related, cooperative sense, or does it simply reflect tradition or the underlying power structure? These and similar questions can be discussed and the appropriate adjustments made.

Admittedly, this case is over-simplified. Still, it makes the essential point that identifying the responsibilities associated with major issues or tasks is imperative. Only then can the need for collaboration and cooperation be determined. Only then can the confusion, conflicts, or gaps in responsibility or authority that detract from cooperative efforts be identified and eliminated.

Once interdependence is noted and areas of necessary cooperation are identified, those who need to work together must communicate and interact with each other effectively. Sound communication, then, is another critical ingredient in creating and sustaining cooperation. Accordingly, we turn our attention to communication in the next chapter.

6

How to Improve Communication

*Communication is vital to cooperation /
What are common obstacles to
communication? / Overcoming the
obstacles to improve communication*

The last chapter focused on determining who must cooperate with whom to get something done. It also emphasized the need to clarify jobs and responsibilities to ensure the success of cooperation. The next critical ingredient for cooperation is communication. There is clearly a need to exchange relevant and timely information among interdependent managers. Without sound communication the teamwork and cooperation needed to sustain a We-Force can never materialize or last within a company.

The obvious need for good communication is surpassed only by the obvious number of communication problems that exist in the real world. In my work with companies over the years, one of the saddest but most common laments or refrains when explaining why something went wrong has been "poor communication." No matter what the problem, more often than not lack of communication is one of the main causes identified by managers.

Poor communication is not merely a convenient whipping boy. Communication is often ineffective, divisive, and injurious to cooperation. Managers occasionally are forced to make important strategic and operating decisions without timely and valid information. At times, decisions makers are burdened by incomplete, irrelevant, even false information.

This chapter reveals why communication is often so poor. It then outlines some steps managers can take to improve communication and, hence, create and sustain cooperation.

Obstacles to Effective Communication

I have encountered a significant number of roadblocks to good communication. Some are more significant and injurious than others, but they all exist and are detrimental to cooperation.

The I-Force. If individual drives and motives are extremely strong, communication around common goals is hardly likely. The harmful competition created by strong individual drives for achievement can militate against shared information and cause hoarding of scarce resources. This behavior affects communication negatively and ultimately destroys cooperation.

The NIH factor. Overzealous rejection of the ideas or decisions of others simply because of the NIH (not invented here) attitude also leads to poor communication and cooperation. Those with NIH syndrome reject help from outsiders and are suspicious about the motives of others. They have an "I can do it better" mentality, which fosters distrust and, ultimately, a breakdown in communication and needed interaction.

Organizational structure. Different functions or divisions can become silos: staunchly independent, vertical organizations that, at best, make lateral communication and cooperation difficult. Division or SBU managers stress autonomy, control over their own dedicated resources, and an emphasis on SBU or divisional performance, not corporate goals. Clearly, these perceptions and goals can negatively affect cooperation when the company needs to increase interdependence and share vital resources across structural units.

Similarly, functional organization can result in a kind of myopia that militates against a corporation-wide view and a feel for the big picture. This inward-looking viewpoint, too, can injure communication and cooperation.

Hierarchy. The greater the number of vertical levels in a hierarchy, the higher the likelihood of communication breakdowns up and down the structural ladder. I once collected data on key aspects of business strategy from top executives, middle managers, and lower-level supervisors in a division of a well-known company. Not surprisingly, top managers felt that strategy and implementation plans were clear and well communicated. Middle managers, and especially the lower echelons, however, did not share the executives' enthusiasm or knowledge. In fact, the lower the position, the more removed the individuals felt and the more negative were their perceptions of communication within the company.

Don't think, however, that hierarchy creates communication problems only between higher and lower levels. Even adjacent levels can have problems communicating and understanding key issues. For example, I remember reading in *The Wall Street Journal*, April 1990, that while eighty-two percent of CEOs felt their strategies were clear and well understood, less than one-third of their vice-presidents and chief operating officers agreed. This finding certainly reveals problems of communication and agreement on key issues, even in the executive suite.

Incentives and performance appraisals. Incentive plans and performance appraisal methods usually keep score by individual achievement, not cooperative performance. Teamwork is often mentioned sanctimoniously but, in reality, is rarely rewarded. Individuals are not promoted because of teamwork, despite its mention as a desirable trait in most performance appraisal systems. This intense focus on individual rewards reduces the perceived importance of shared communication and cooperation, at best. At worst, the emphasis on individual performance and recognition undermines communication and motivates managers to manipulate, hoard, or control information, not share it for the common good.

Organizational culture. One company I worked with for years had a large number of SBUs. Each was an independent profit center, totally self-contained around its products and market. Over time, the company developed a culture of rugged individualism and entrepreneurship, valued assets in most situations.

But market and customer needs began to change. Customers, for example, began to reject the role of integrators. Large customers that routinely bought products from many different SBUs began to resent the extra time and work needed to coordinate different suppliers, all of which were from the same company. Customers wanted to talk to one representative supplier, not legions of different suppliers.

In brief, the market wanted the company to do the integrating.

Consequently, coordination was defined as the responsibility of new group-level managers working with a number of SBUs. The company felt that such a change was logical and simple. Moreover, top management expected that the SBU heads would welcome group-level help with the integration problem.

This was not the case, however. Integration, at best, was poorly done and problematical. Why? Because of the entrenched culture of entrepreneurship and individualism in the SBUs. Coordination by increased centralization was rejected in a predominantly decentralized organization. SBU managers did not share information readily or cooperate with the new group-level "bureaucrats," and the hoped-for communication and coordination across business units never materialized. Individual goals and perceptions of autonomy created a cultural resistance to change and proved extremely difficult to overcome. What were clearly rational goals and perceptions at one level proved to be contrary to the culture at another.

Most managers reading the preceding examples easily can contribute many more of their own cases of poor communication. However, instead of dwelling on the problems, let's tackle the obstacles head on and discuss ways to improve communication and cooperation. Below I present a number of steps that, taken together, will encourage the We-Force and the cooperation it thrives on.

Tackle Obvious Barriers First

Many companies have obvious communication barriers that can be tackled first. They are not always easy barriers to remove. Still, they represent a good starting point around which to rally attention and support.

Common Language

As difficult as it is to believe, managers within the same company sometimes speak different languages! While they all may be speaking English within the company or within divisions in different countries, their jargon, symbols, or data create almost Babel-like confusion of terms and "tongues" that detracts heavily from communication and teamwork.

Good communication and cooperation need commonly understood language, symbols, systems, and priorities. They also depend on common beliefs and values that underlie and support interactions and communications.

A company I know well went through a period in which it tried to "flatten" or "delayer" the organization. The purpose was to eliminate layers, bureaucracy, and unnecessary positions, while simultaneously fostering delegation, communication, and interaction. Actual results, however, were far from happy and useful. As one person explained it:

> Spans of control increased tremendously due to the virtual elimination of an entire level. Of necessity, our company had to become more decentralized. Getting help from the boss is possible when span of control is one to seven; it's virtually impossible when span is one to forty-nine or some such ridiculous number!
>
> Decentralization, in turn, meant that we, this group of forty-nine, had to communicate laterally, with each other, rather than go through our bosses as we did in the past. Only then did we realize that so many things were different across units. The beliefs, values, and operating principles were simply not the same, due to past differences in goals, competition, and history of the units. One group talked about margins, contribution, real costs, and value-added measurements that were foreign to people in other units. Perceptions of profit varied, as different groups subtracted different expenses to arrive at different net figures. One group mentioned customers' needs frequently, while another had never seen or talked to customers, hence, couldn't care less about them. There literally was nothing in common to bind people who previously had different bosses and views of the world. A common outlook to help the restructuring was not present.
>
> With so little in common, it was extremely difficult to communicate. I know it sounds unbelievable, being the same company and all that, but it's true. We couldn't talk to each other!

Common language—terms, symbols, systems, procedures, values, and so on—facilitates communication. Focusing first on this obvious need is a critical step in fostering cooperation and teamwork.

What can managers do to develop a common language? Some of the answers have been provided in earlier chapters.

1. A first step is to create a statement of vision or mission. It

helps to discuss what the company, SBU, or department is all about. A credo or mission bonds people with something in common, sets the stage for a consistent language or set of meaningful symbols, and generates organization-wide agreement on what the vision means.

2. It is useful to locate points of interdependence to determine who must work together. Interdependence and its task orientation then can drive the development of a common language among those who must interact and communicate to achieve results.

3. The steps above imply the critical need to generate agreement on vision, tasks, responsibilities, and performance measures that reflect the collective effort. A logical, related step is to agree on the data, information, and common language that will be used to communicate what is happening as a result of the collective effort. In service organizations, for example, different units must agree on the definition of important outcomes, like overall quality and customer satisfaction, as well as each unit's contribution to those outcomes. The purpose of this step is to force people to define or operationalize what is being worked on and how the results will be monitored and measured. Discussion of agreed-upon measures facilitates communication, and the measures themselves are tools of communication.

4. Finally, if needed, a glossary of common terms or definitions can be developed to avoid semantic problems and facilitate understanding. It is much easier for division managers in New York, Sao Paulo, and Amsterdam to talk about ROI and SBU performance with corporate or headquarters managers if the definition of investment and measures of return are commonly understood and agreed upon.

In essence, it's necessary to look for what's needed in common and to pursue it. Alternatively, it is useful to focus on differences and discrepancies and eliminate them. A common language and view are critical to communication and cooperation.

Eliminate Geographical Barriers to Communication

People who must cooperate should be as close together physically as possible. Geographical dispersion negatively affects performance under conditions of high interdependence.

A number of years ago, I was working with a company concerned with product realignment and new product development. The goal was to find new markets for existing products, and/or develop products for new markets. To facilitate the process, the company had set up a number of development teams. At the end of the first year, a couple of teams had performed well, another couple had performed rather dismally, and the rest were somewhere in the middle.

Working closely with management, a colleague and I attempted to explain the great divergence in performance between the low and high groups. Many factors were considered, of course. But one day early on, something obvious jumped out of the analysis: members of the two high-performing teams were at or in close proximity to corporate headquarters, whereas the members of low-performing groups were spread all over the country or globe. Geographical dispersion made communication and cooperation much more difficult. Under conditions of high interdependence, geographical diversity hurts communication and performance, while physical proximity is essential to cooperative effort.

What must be done? Rethink the teams. As much as is feasible, create groups in which individuals have access to each other. If geographical differences cannot be eliminated, make sure substitute methods of communication and interaction are available (e.g., telecommunication methods). Assign responsibility to integrators, key managers whose job it is to coordinate and communicate team activities. Measure the consequences of cooperation and communication, and reward people for the results. It's not easy to coordinate activities that are broadly dispersed, but it's worth the effort.

Reduce or Eliminate Administrative Barriers to Cooperation

Speed and timeliness in the innovation or product development process, for example, are often adversely affected by administrative bottlenecks. Those attempting to cooperate must go through channels, get numerous approvals, and undergo frequent checks and controls, all of which slow the process and make communication and cooperation a burden.

In a similar vein, those attempting something new in traditional areas often must get permission to walk on sacred ground. Getting permission, however, frequently is no easy task. It often demands justification of the new methods—for example, how bills are paid, how much investment can be made by SBU managers without corporate review, or who orders supplies. At worst, managers don't bother communicating and justifying new methods because of the effort and bureaucratic hurdles they would face. At best, the process of change proceeds at a tortoise-like pace. Getting permission also reinforces a hierarchical system that can result in the premature veto of ideas and projects. Some managers still take a risk and do what they want because, as one manager aptly put it, "It is much easier to seek forgiveness after the fact than get permission before it."

Communication and interaction clearly could be served better if management sought out and eliminated these common administrative stumbling blocks. The real question is how to identify the obstacles and eliminate them.

An ideal process for this task has already been discussed and outlined in chapter 4—the nominal-group technique. Following the steps laid out in the appendix of that chapter, managers would choose a target goal, for example, improving the product development process, facilitating communication across functions, and so on. Data would be collected from the group on the obstacles or roadblocks to that process. Priorities would be set, with the major obstacles identified and agreed upon via the voting process outlined. Steps for remedial action would be planned, and the appropriate follow-up or control measures would be instituted to guarantee problem solution.

This approach to decision-making or problem solving is extremely useful in many situations, including the elimination of communication problems and administrative obstacles to company action.

Delegation

Delegation can aid communication and teamwork immensely. It implies trust and confidence, which can motivate managers to interact with others to handle problems. Delegation and the authority it implies also eliminate the need to always get permission from someone higher up in the company. The freedom to decide and act certainly is more conducive to communication, cooperation, and action than most formal processes of seeking and giving approvals.

Delegation also carries with it considerable responsibility. Delegation implies empowerment and an emphasis on results, which motivates people to meet their responsibilities and accomplish the task at hand. This motivation to perform often generates positive efforts to communicate and coordinate to get the job done.

A final obvious obstacle to communication is poor advertising. Not in the usual sense directed to an external market, but rather, internal advertising.

By All Means, Advertise!

An extremely basic but surprisingly prevalent reason for lack of communication and cooperation is simply the fact that people don't know whom to contact to seek help or request services.

> Well, I'm not exactly sure who to call on this one. It could be marketing, or even engineering, because customer specs are involved. Marketing would probably be the place to call. Yeah, get on the horn to marketing.

This situation in this real example created two types of problem that slowed management's response. First, the people involved didn't know which functional area had the main responsibility for the issue at hand (see chapter 4). The second problem emerged later when someone raised a few simple questions:

> Call marketing? What do you mean, "call marketing?" Who? Do I get on the phone and say, "Yo, marketing, solve my problem!"? Who is marketing? How do I keep from getting bounced from person to person until someone decides my problem is within his job jurisdiction?

Communication begins with knowledge, including knowing who does what, when, and why. Communication depends on knowing the people with the expertise to help in a particular matter. The confusion in the preceding example is all too commonplace, but it is easily eliminated with good advertising. How does one advertise? As a corporate executive in a bank holding company once told me:

I know a head of MIS in a regional bank who advertised very effective-ly. After a period of study and analysis, he sent out information packets showing what the central MIS function could do more efficiently than any of the branches. He showed how he could save them time, grief, and money. The information packet noted the people to call on specif-ic issues or for particular kinds of help. A personal touch was added—peoples' familiar names or nicknames were listed. This led to fewer ob-stacles to calling, as individuals in the branches didn't feel they were contacting an impersonal, centralized bureau of some sort. I know the idea is simple, but, boy, was it effective.

Advertising in this case worked beautifully. The branches were happy with the customized service. MIS grew and became more central, much to the delight of the head of that function. Overall, the managers both at the home office and in the field talked about good communication and a win-win situation. Advertising had gen-erated critical information and a personal touch in an area general-ly marked by gross impersonality.

Advertising, then, is communication in that it provides valuable information about responsibilities, expertise, and the people who perform necessary tasks. Further, it fosters additional communica-tion, as managers see fewer obstacles and less wasted time and ef-fort because they now know whom to call for what help. This facil-itation of communication obviously boosts cooperation.

Develop Good Information

Having just mentioned MIS, it is appropriate to focus next on the critical impact of information on communication and a We-Force.

Communication and cooperation cannot survive without good information. Good information is timely, relevant data applicable to a decision or task at hand. It is directly relevant to the manage-ment tactics being tried ("this technology or structure should create efficiency and a reduction in cost per unit"), and allows for a valid testing of them. Good information is timely because it allows com-panies to be flexible and adapt to changing market conditions. Sound information builds managerial confidence in its own ability to plan, especially for the long term.

Unfortunately, sometimes companies don't have good information. Instead, they have bad or irrelevant information, which negatively affects decisions and, ultimately, a desire to communicate and cooperate. Why isn't this obvious need for good information met? There are, I believe, at least three possible explanations.

The first reason is that the organization hasn't thought out what constitutes good information. Managers simply know that data and information exist; they never question whether the information is appropriate or helpful.

I was involved once in a project with a large federal government agency. Part of my job was to consider the best ways to organize field offices when efficiency was the prime performance criterion. I recommended a functional-type organization because of its emphasis on repetition, task specialization, volume, and avoidance of duplication. I expected variable cost per case to decrease.

To test the hypothesis, good information on costs was vital. I requested information on variable costs, but was told, "We don't have cost breakdowns like that. Let me show you what we have. We have figures totaled every month that show total cost for each field office. You'll have to use these figures. This is what we have."

The problem was that the information available did not allow for a valid testing of the theory. The total cost figure they wanted to use included fixed costs (mortgages, leases, building depreciation, etc.) that had nothing to do with the expected relationship between structure and cost per case. The information was not useful.

After a period of persuasion, argument, and discussion, I finally got someone to revisit the computer software and create a very simple program to identify and add up the appropriate variable costs per month. Only then could communication and cooperation occur. Only then could we all see and analyze the real relationships between structure and costs.

The point is that the initial reaction was: "Here, this is what we have. Use it. Whether good or bad, this is what we've collected. Use it the best way you can." This type of insistence on using bad information can hurt communication and cooperation, besides generating poor results.

The second explanation for poor information is somewhat related to the previous one, but it is sufficiently different to warrant separate attention. The problem here stems from the MIS group and is succinctly summarized in a statement I heard Russ Ackoff make:[1]

"Most managers do not suffer from a lack of relevant information. Rather, most managers suffer from an overabundance of irrelevant information."

A typical scenario involving MIS plays like this. Some department or function seeks information to analyze a problem. The parameters of the problem aren't very clear yet, but managers need information to begin crystallizing the key issues. MIS receives their request, but isn't sure what data the managers need. To be safe, then, MIS sends them everything. When in doubt, don't pick and chose. A core dump of everything that could be relevant is the safest thing to do: send everything, and let them sort out what they need.

This strategy, of course, creates problems. The good information, if any, is buried. Requests for clarification or priorities are met by MIS with, "Hey, you wanted the stuff and we gave it to you. What you do with it now is your problem." It is easy to see how future communication and cooperation between the groups could suffer or deteriorate.

The third reason for a lack of valid and timely information is simply that managers don't tell the truth. They bias the information or even lie. There is no incentive to pass on valuable data. Indeed, the incentive might be to pass on worthless information. A classic case is when a company has a habit of killing the messenger when bad news is communicated. Because of all-too-frequent messenger deaths, the company guarantees that only good news is transmitted.

The habit of killing the messenger ensures poor, biased information. It also kills good communication. Cooperation is extremely difficult, at best, because political games, excessive conservatism, and covering one's butt are the operational norms. Good communication and cooperation cannot exist under conditions of fear and the consequent censoring of information.

To foster good communication and cooperation, you must focus on three things:

- *Know the specific information necessary for your task.* A detailed analysis is the first step.
- *Operationalize what you need.* Knowing that information is needed on service "excellence" or "quality" is not sufficient. Ways to measure and operationalize those variables must be accomplished

as a second step to allow transmittal of the right information. Using customer feedback or opinion surveys as measures of quality service places different demands on information collection and processing than the use of market share data or trends in product substitution by customers as measures of quality.

• *Eliminate fear and distrust.* Managers must not be afraid to transmit valid information. Killing messengers who bring negative information kills honesty and valid information. Communication and cooperation cannot thrive under conditions of fear or distrust. Eliminating this atmosphere of paranoia is vital in creating and sustaining good communication and the cooperative efforts so vital to a We-Force.

Think Teams

Another positive step that fosters good communication is to use teams effectively. The key word here is effectively. Ineffective use of teams creates problems and negatively affects communication and cooperation. Ineffective teams, among other things, are set up for the wrong reasons; are too large; are politically motivated; have no clear sense of task; avoid decisions at all costs; avoid responsibility or blame, especially in unpopular matters; and have no common, superordinate goals to bind and unify efforts.

In contrast, viable teams are set up only when necessary—e.g., under conditions of reciprocal interdependence. They are not set up to rubber stamp the decisions of others. In an effective team, all of the members clearly understand the task, the time frame for completion, and how the composition of the group is related to the task.

An effective team's responsibility and authority are clearly spelled out. Whether its role is advisory (e.g., suggesting possible options in some order of preference) or whether it has the authority to decide an issue, the team's role must be clarified up front. This prerequisite prevents inappropriate expectations and communication difficulties down the road.

Controls should be set up for team performance, including reporting requirements. The time frame for decision making and reporting of milestones also must be agreed upon. These steps guarantee discussion and communication of key issues and avert some of the problems typically associated with groups (e.g., stalling for time, "paralysis through analysis," and so on).

Teams can be effective operating tools for communication. Cross-functional groups can solve sticky problems of coordination. Through team building, a synergistic environment and a culture based on agreement and cooperation can become realities.

Manage Laterally

Managing laterally, or "thinking sideways," in organizations can facilitate communication. This step was touched on when discussing interdependence, but it is worth additional attention.

Most managers think vertically more than laterally. Concern is more often with a boss's demands or subordinates' activities than with the problems or concerns of others not in one's span of control or chain of command. Thinking sideways focuses attention on communication and coordination quite differently than vertical thinking does.

Consider the case, again, of a company losing customers because of poor product quality. Vertical thinking usually causes entrenchment. Protective walls are erected as individuals within the vertical structure or silo are concerned with covering themselves at all costs. Views laterally only include finger-pointing and laying blame on others for the problem. Communication clearly suffers.

> Hell, we did our jobs, we pulled our weight. Don't blame us for the problem. You'd be much better off looking for the answer over in engineering or testing. Didn't we warn you that this was bound to happen?

Thinking sideways forces a different view. The Deming method is a good example of thinking laterally to identify and solve problems.[2] Deming defines a very simple process model that looks something like the one in figure 6.1. Forced with a loss of customers due to poor quality, what would happen? Customer feedback would be examined, as would the performance of the processing system (technology, communication, managerial coordination, etc.) within the company. The customer would be part of the deliberations. So would those from different functions within the company responsible for quality. External suppliers might also be involved or be con-

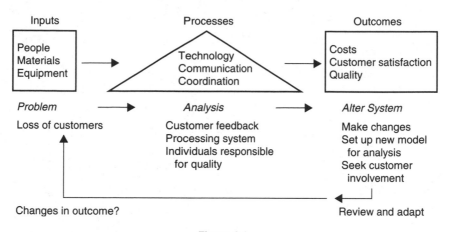

Figure 6.1

sulted. The goal of the search process would be to actively seek opportunities to improve things, not to lay blame.

Once a way to improve quality has been identified, those involved would test their theory. New processes would be added or changed within the processing system. The new results would be observed and the significance of changes in performance noted. Commitment to the new ways of doing things would be sought if the tests showed that the changes were viable. Emphasis would be on communication, agreement, cooperation, and, ultimately, customer satisfaction.

Managing laterally, then, is concerned with the entire value-added chain, the big picture. It forces individuals in different areas to think of superordinate goals, like quality and customer satisfaction. Thinking laterally emphasizes the importance of communication and cooperation in reaching goals and making the system work. The focus is on the whole, not just the needs of the parts.

All of the efforts to improve and facilitate communication noted so far are important. Many would go for naught, however, without this last step: setting up incentive and control systems that reward and reinforce the right behaviors, actions, and results.

Good communication and teamwork will not occur if they are not rewarded. The issue of incentives, rewards, and controls is vital to a full understanding of how to motivate and sustain cooperation. This is our concern in the next chapter.

7

Above All,
Reward the Right Things

Reward cooperation / Reinforce teamwork

Setting up appropriate incentives and controls is the most important factor in creating and sustaining cooperation. The problem
is that incentive systems frequently recognize only individual performance and neglect or ignore cooperation and teamwork. As two
managers recently reminded me:

> Stars get ahead around here, not constellations.

> The mission statement says "we." The company vision statement and
> list of guiding principles says "we." But performance appraisal, promo-
> tion, and pay raises call for "I," "me," or "mine." We nod approvingly
> when we hear "us," but we go off and worry about "me."

Rewards are feedback; they tell people what's important. Incentives and controls reinforce certain outcomes or behaviors, and
they cause people to neglect or reject others. Hoping for an essential behavior such as cooperation is not sufficient to produce it. The
right rewards and reinforcement are critical to getting what you
want. Simply put, you get what you pay for. People will not work
in the manner you desire unless they are recognized, rewarded, and
reinforced.

Rewards like compensation and promotion provide incentives to
perform in certain ways. But incentives and controls transcend formal rewards. They include other forms of feedback and informal
guidelines about what is acceptable or desirable performance in a

company. Top management's approvals, disapprovals, and stated preferences motivate and control subordinates' performance as assuredly as formal reward systems.

Make Sure You Have Good Incentives

Good incentives reward the right behavior. They motivate performance that is consistent with desired outcomes. Determining the desired outcomes is the result of planning, communication, generation of agreement, and other processes discussed in previous chapters.

Bad incentives almost always are coercive or negative. Some typical statements from managers I've heard over the years emphasize the point clearly.

> "You'd better make the number, or you're gone."
> "Your reward for doing a good job today is that you get to come back and try again tomorrow."
> "Help [another function]? Why? Make them look good? Hell, no way! We help them, they get more bucks and we get screwed."
> "Mess up once around here and you're in trouble. Better to lie low, just get by, and don't attract any attention, because it usually turns out bad."

As these statements suggest, coercive or negative feedback usually brings out the worst in people. The emphasis is on avoiding mistakes, not on doing things better. Innovation and creativity involve risk taking and increase the probability of mistakes as one experiments with novel approaches to problem solving. If incentives and controls are coercive and force people not to make mistakes, innovation and risk taking, including new forms of cooperative ventures, will not occur.

Generally, good incentives are positive and come in two types: *utilitarian* and *psychological*. The first type includes things of extrinsic value (pay, bonus, salary, promotion), while the second is more intrinsic or personal (psychological identification, a feeling of doing what's right, having fun with work, and autonomy). Many rewards smack of both, as when a manager receives a pat on the back or visible recognition for work well done. Certainly the visible pat bodes well for promotion or a healthy raise in salary. But it also feels good, enhancing the self-image and confidence of the individual receiving it.

Good incentives, then, usually include both utilitarian and psychological rewards. They are not given arbitrarily or capriciously, but are tied to agreed-upon measures of performance, as I stress later. Good incentive plans encourage the right managerial motivations and behaviors and channel individual efforts toward the common goals central to a We-Force.

Proper incentives do not injure cooperation, nor do they foster situations leading to suboptimization for a company. A recent case provides an example of these injurious effects. Three divisions of a company refused to share their knowledge, skills, or technology for the benefit of the entire corporation. Each division was motivated to hoard resources and protect its proprietary expertise so it could beat the other divisions in the competition for funding and larger shares of the bonus pool. Although sharing knowledge and capabilities would have created an opportunity for synergy and scale economies, cooperation and joint efforts were avoided. The incentive system motivated managers to be concerned with SBU performance, not with what was best for the entire company in a highly competitive industry.

When I pointed this suboptimization out to the three SBU heads, their responses were virtually identical. They saw cooperation as risky. Each felt that the other two would ostensibly play along with an offer to cooperate, but in the final analysis would somehow take advantage of the "naive" manager to better their own positions.

Why do such incentive and control anomalies occur? How can managers use incentives to ensure cooperation and joint decision making?

Saying You Want One Thing, While Rewarding Another

One of the biggest and most common problems with incentives in many companies is that they reward the wrong behavior or result. Managers say they are working toward one objective, but the system rewards another. When the desired outcome or activity is mentioned, managers nod approvingly. Despite the agreement and the nodding, however, managers go off and pursue totally different outcomes. Unfortunately, this problem is common across companies and industries.

The examples are endless. A company's planning process or annual report emphasizes product or service quality as the focus of future efforts. Much is made of quality as the linchpin of future competitive success. In practice, however, managers are constantly pressured to reduce costs. Cost saving becomes the driving force. Managers believe that not achieving lower costs will get them into trouble. Thus the drive for cost reduction hurts product or service quality. The company ostensibly wants quality, but clearly is rewarding economy.

One company I worked with wanted increased innovation in certain critical areas. Innovation, of course, usually demands cooperation. It also requires experimentation before new ideas or solutions are discovered, tested, and tried successfully. This company's culture, however, was marked by conservatism and risk avoidance, which created an interesting dilemma. As one manager put it:

> The company tells me to innovate. The big guys preach innovation at our annual fling, the planning meeting. My boss says innovation is good. I tell my boss I'll have to experiment, spend a few bucks, etc. In effect, I've got to take some risks in order to innovate. So my boss says, "Take all the risk you want—just be right!" So you know what I do, right? Exactly! I do nothing.

In another case, a large government agency had developed an agency-wide program to achieve client satisfaction and a high-quality response to client complaints. The strategy ostensibly placed clients at the core of a social services network, with their needs as the prime generator of other actions and support services.

As a result of increased service to clients, however, professional contact hours and administrative support time increased markedly, causing a significant jump in overtime expense and support activities. Higher authorities in the government bureaucracy soon noted the increased costs with alarm. Eventually, feedback on the performance of all the agency's units and programs included a heavy emphasis on the need for cost controls. Justifications for deviations from budget were demanded routinely. Performance appraisals for the heads of agency departments began to focus heavily on performance against budgeted costs.

Despite documented increases in client satisfaction, the new programs eventually were modified to reduce costs. Client-related efforts predictably became secondary to cost-reduction. Staff dissatisfaction increased significantly as the emphasis on clients desired by the professionals was overruled by an agency program supported by bureaucrats. The message was clear: client satisfaction is important and desirable, but only if costs don't increase.

It's not only companies and the government that ask for one result but reward another. The hallowed halls of academia often are just as self-defeating. Consider a proposal I saw to upgrade an MBA curriculum. The new curriculum was intended to improve teamwork and cooperation among students. However, there were no plans to alter the existing grading curve, according to which only a fixed percent of students could get the highest grade and a certain percent had to flunk. The school was hoping for teamwork, but it was fostering competition and a win-lose mentality.

I could list dozens of additional examples of organizations hoping for one outcome but rewarding quite another. It is foolish and often debilitating to say that something is indispensable only to turn around and reward something else. *Organizations always get what they pay for.* Good incentive plans follow this simple rule when cooperation is the desired result.

Actions Speak Louder Than Words

Managers, especially top management, can motivate subordinates' behavior by setting a good example. Most employees see and understand much of what's going on, even in the executive suite. Moreover, they often look to management for guidance, especially in gray areas dealing with ethics, appropriate competitive behavior, and interpretations of official policy.

Not long ago I was working in Japan with a high-ranking manager in an automotive company. Somehow, the group discussion turned to the subject of vacations. The manager, who was trying to pull off a major strategic maneuver, offered his view. "In the past two years, I have taken only two vacation days. How can I expect my people to work hard and dedicate themselves to the task at hand if I don't provide a good example for them to follow?"

Many of us may not entirely agree with this manager's workaholic viewpoint, but there's no question about the message he's sending. Actions speak louder than words. If innovation and risk taking are sought within the company, managers must exhibit innovative actions. If ethical standards are important, managers cannot ask others to conform to them until they themselves exhibit ethical behavior. If accepting responsibility is desired at lower ranks, managers must delegate. More importantly, upon delegating, they must not immediately crush managers who take risks and make mistakes. The last point raises the question of rewards and performance appraisal.

Reward Teamwork and Cooperation

Coordinating Goals and Incentives

Cooperation, if desired, should be recognized. Yet many companies only reward individual behavior and performance. Incentives and positive feedback are rarely based on cooperative efforts. In some cases I've observed, managers are rewarded for climbing over the bodies of colleagues, not working with them. Companies must reward cooperation and reinforce the behaviors that go with it.

For example, a new product development team should be rewarded as a team for product development. A bonus, if awarded, would go to the team. Let members decide among themselves who gets what share. Or, while SBU managers should be paid for SBU performance, part of the bonus could be given on the basis of overall corporate performance. Under these circumstances, the SBU managers will worry more about collective effort and superordinate goals. At minimum, they won't do only what's good for their SBUs if it means hurting managers in other SBUs or functions. At least they'll think twice about it! Similarly, production managers will be much more reluctant to shrug off customer dissatisfaction if a portion of their pay is tied to measures of customer satisfaction. Upon hearing about the loss of a major account, they won't say "it's marketing's problem" when their own income is at risk.Or, to take an example from academia, MBA students will worry only about themselves if the grading curve results in forced flunkings. Win-lose situations breed the perception that self-interest must be first and foremost. To foster cooperation, emphasis must be on joint projects and the fact that everyone wins if the team does well. All of these examples show that common incentives spark common concerns. They foster cooperation around superordinate goals.

Teamwork can be hard to measure or operationalize, and not many companies have focused on doing so. Still, until the effort is made to define and recognize teamwork, cooperative efforts will happen only by chance. Two critical questions must be answered in order to define teamwork and its results. How does one recognize the need for cooperative goals and actions? How, then, does one measure and operationalize outcomes related to teamwork and not just individual performance?

The first answer is found in chapters 4 and 5 on planning and managing interdependence. Under reciprocal interdependence, for example, goals cannot be achieved by the independent, uncoordinated actions of individuals. Indeed, individually directed behavior and goals can be harmful to joint decision making and results. Communication and face-to-face interaction are vital to problem solving, and coordination is by mutual adjustment as interdependent managers adapt to task-related issues. Objectives in this case represent superordinate goals that can result only from cooperative action. The type of interdependence, then, defines the need for cooperation and teamwork.

Similarly, the responsibility matrix can help to identify the people essential to the joint effort. Delegation of authority and assignment of responsibilities to achieve common, superordinate goals follow logically from this analysis of roles. The need for cooperative action is clarified by the assignment of jobs in the responsibility matrix.

These initial analyses also generate agreement or consensus on the critical outcomes of cooperative action. Agreement breeds a commitment to identify and develop good measures of performance, which paves the way for the next critical task: how actually to operationalize and measure key performance objectives that relate to cooperation and joint efforts.

Measuring the Results of Cooperation

Cooperation is a characteristic of decision making. It can also be defined as a desired outcome in itself, as when a manager asserted to me that his organization "strives for teamwork above all other results." For cooperation to be taken seriously, however, and for the We-Force to survive, the outcomes of cooperation must be stipulated and operationalized. Only then can desired performance be recognized, tracked, and reinforced.

Consider, again, the SBU managers who nod approvingly when cooperation is mentioned, but still relentlessly pursue only individual, not collective, measures of performance. A missing ingredient here is the clear definition of the results of cooperation and the consequent forging of a link between results and reward. Cooperation supposedly results in synergy across SBUs, for instance, but what is synergy and how does one know when it's been attained?

The presence of synergy can be defined by proxy measures. These measures include, but are not limited to:

- Economies of scale or scope.
- More productive R&D efforts, with new products, services, or technologies reflecting the cooperation and efficiency of joint SBU ventures.
- Increased corporate sales, if effectiveness is due to the integration of disparate customer needs across markets served by the SBUs.
- Increased company, not SBU, profitability, on the assumption that cooperative efforts foster the goals of the whole, not its parts.
- Increased company stock price over time, as an efficient market recognizes and places values on financial results and a long-term prognosis of success from a coordinated strategy toward markets or customers.

Once the outcomes of cooperation are stipulated and measurable, it is possible to affix rewards to their accomplishment. Only then will SBU managers do more than nod approvingly at the prospects of working together for the common good. Teamwork can also be measured by any of the objectives developed through the methods explained in chapter 4.

A company can take a number of steps to create and sustain cooperation. Some deal with incentives directly, some indirectly through controls or feedback, but all deal with recognition, reinforcement, and reward. Most are under the control of individual managers, and all are important to creating and sustaining a We-Force in an organization. A good example is that of performance appraisal and its impact on cooperation.

Revise Performance Appraisal and Review Methods

Most traditional performance appraisal and review (PA&R) systems destroy teamwork, pit individuals against each other, and promote mediocrity or excessive homogeneity. They can destroy risk taking, change, and innovation, while encouraging people to play it safe or maintain the status quo.

Consider, for example, the very common forced-ranking methods of PA&R. Driven by an ill-conceived notion of a normal distribution, managers believe that abilities are normally distributed within a company—that is, they fall along a bell-shaped curve. PA&R methods, it is believed, can be based on this so-called fact. Accordingly, a manager with ten subordinates is told that, when doing PA&R, only two subordinates can be ranked as outstanding, only three as above average, and three as average; the remaining two must be below average.

The scientific reasoning underlying the use of such PA&R methods is usually wrong. If randomly selected and large enough, a sample of people will reflect the distribution of characteristics normally found in a population. However, no company that I know of randomly chooses its personnel from an undifferentiated population of potential candidates (despite some managers' protestations to the contrary).

More importantly, use of forced ranking is divisive at best and totally destructive of cooperation at worst. It pits manager against manager for the favorable rankings. The system dictates that there must be winners and losers, even if all managers are nearly identical in skills and performance capabilities.

Desire to avoid the below-average category leads to other dysfunctional behavior, such as subordinates promoting the hiring of marginally capable or even unqualified people rather than stars. Their boss wants stars to improve departmental performance, but subordinates aren't rewarded for overall performance; they're more concerned about their jobs. Poor ratings also lead to severe morale problems. Not only do some people have to deal with being ranked as below average, they also may know that they are better than someone in a neighboring department who got an above-average rating.

Other foolish and detrimental outcomes can occur. Individuals may try to transfer to other departments because they can do better where there's weaker competition. Obviously, there is no motivation to work within a group of bright people who collectively could create amazing synergies and do outstanding things for a company. Cooperation suffers further, as only individual achievements form the basis for the PA&R and resultant rewards.

Poor PA&R methods injure both individual motivation and cooperative behaviors, so good methods clearly have additional benefits beyond supporting the We-Force. Sound PA&R techniques are vital to organizational performance and morale.

What should PA&R look like? If forced rankings and similar methods are counterproductive, what attributes would a good system have? What can individual managers and their companies do to create cooperation?

First, the focus of PA&R should not be solely on individual goals, as traditionally has been the case. PA&R also should be based on measures of performance that can be accomplished only via cooperative efforts.

The preferred approach forces managers to think of interdependence, cooperation, and the results of joint efforts. I once was involved with a highly successful experiment in a global chemical company. The company wished to emphasize product development—both new products and new markets for existing products— a very difficult chore in a commodity business. To achieve the desired outcome, a number of steps were taken.

1. Planning suggested high levels of task interdependence around product development objectives. Effective communication and coordination across functions were deemed vital to finding and serving new customers, designing and manufacturing new lines, and revamping or retooling existing products. Seven teams were set up in recognition of these needs.
2. Performance milestones were defined as team objectives. Emphasis was on measuring the overall outcomes of cooperative effort—for example, penetration of new market segments,

with penetration defined in terms of revenues, number of customers, and market share.

3. The distinction between individual and cooperative objectives was delineated clearly for purposes of evaluation and PA&R. A manager or technical specialist had both individual and team objectives. The percentage of time and effort to be directed toward individual and team objectives was discussed and agreed upon up front. Future PA&R, it was decided, would be based equally on individual and team outcomes.

4. Actual PA&R was consistent with the previously agreed-upon guidelines and conditions. PA&R was based equally on an individual's performance on personal objectives and the team's overall performance on collective milestones and objectives.

5. Financial rewards based on team performance were given to the team. Members then decided, within the team, how the overall pot was to be distributed. This step was vitally important because it signaled the significance of the team in matters of control and the equitable distribution of rewards. A formula for evaluation was not forced on the team, for evaluation and feedback are best done by those directly involved in the task.

The results of the experiment were significant, both in terms of company performance and managerial attitudes. By defining both individual and team goals and then basing PA&R on them, the message became increasingly clear: cooperative efforts are important. Pay and recognition depend, in part, on joint efforts and outcomes, not just individual achievement.

In sum, PA&R must recognize, operationalize, and legitimize cooperative efforts and joint decision making. Otherwise, companies may be hard-pressed to attain the level of cooperation and success needed to survive in an increasingly competitive future.

As a second step toward fostering cooperation through the PA&R process, care must be taken to avoid all-or-nothing objectives that create destructively competitive win-lose situations.

All-or-nothing objectives force the question, of a person or group, "did you make the objective or not?" Degrees of performance are not possible, just mutually exclusive performance categories, usually "good" and "bad" performance.

It is easy to see how cooperation can suffer when PA&R is an either-or proposition. To ensure good performance, individuals, SBUs, teams, or functions may hoard scarce resources and refuse to share important knowledge and skills with others. Cooperation will not occur under these conditions because the motivation is to look good or make others look bad in the PA&R process.

All-or-nothing objectives force managers to low-ball to ensure winning instead of losing. They foster mediocrity. Managers and teams will not perform too well, even if the opportunity presents itself. After all, what will next year's objectives be if a manager or group breaks the curve this year? Generally speaking, win-lose objectives demand that people focus on survival and thus destroy teamwork and cooperation.

It is imperative, then, to avoid defining all-or-nothing objectives. Performance must be judged by employing relative measures of performance, not mutually exclusive good and bad categories.

Consider again the case of the product development teams in the chemical company. Seven teams were set up, and each had its own objectives in terms of new products or markets. In no instance were a team's objectives treated as an all-or-nothing proposition. PA&R was not based on whether or not a team reached a desired level of performance. Instead, degrees of performance relative to objectives were calculated and discussed.

The definition or operationalization of objectives obviously is critical here. In this case, the team's objectives included:

• The number of new products relative to budget (output per dollar of input).
• Market share and revenues gained per new product.
• New market share and revenues relative to budget.
• Patents applied for and awarded as a result of team effort.
• The number of new customers gained from the development effort.
• A "potentiality" score for each new product and market, derived by agreed-upon experts in the company, that measured the potential long-term benefits to the company from product development.

PA&R across the teams reflected performance against the preceding objectives, and the teams were evaluated relative to each other. The PA&R was not an all-or-nothing proposition in which some teams won and others lost. Instead, comparing new product development performance resulted in a distribution of the teams on percentage of the objectives achieved, as shown in figure 7.1.

In the distribution of compensation, teams 1 and 7 received the largest bonus, teams 3 and 4 the smallest, and teams 5, 2, and 6 something in between the maximum and minimum. The important point is twofold: each team got something that reflected its contribution to the company, and PA&R clearly was tied to agreed-upon measures of performance.

These two points bring us to our last prescription regarding PA&R. For effective PA&R, the methods and data of evaluation, how actual and desired performance are to be compared, and the links between performance and reward should be clear and agreed upon up front.

If an indivisual or team is not to be evaluated on completion of the objective alone, but also on completion compared to some industry or competitor average, then this standard must be clear and agreed upon. Similarly, the basis for relative comparisons among managers or teams in a division or across divisions in a company must be delineated and operationalized. The links between rewards and performance then can be forged consistently and unequivocally.

The point of this prescription is that expectations and methods of PA&R must be clarified before the performance and evaluation occur. Without such a clarification, people can come up with all sorts of measures after the fact to prove how well they really performed. This revisionism often generates disagreements, bad feelings, and a climate disruptive to cooperation and superordinate goals. Effective PA&R clarifies expectations, goals, and evaluation measures and methods in advance to avoid such disruptions.

In sum, emphasis must be on PA&R as a cooperative effort, with both the methods or techniques of appraisal and the appraisal itself

**Team Performance in Terms of
Objectives Achieved**

0% of		3, 4	5, 2, 6	1, 7		100% of
Objectives			50%			Objectives

Figure 7.1

reflecting communication, agreement, and cooperation. The goal is to eliminate a win-lose mentality and create the win-win situation so vital to a We-Force. This goal cannot be achieved, however, until the results of cooperation are clearly measured, their benefit to the organization visibly acknowledged, and their contribution to PA&R recognized by all involved.

Eliminate Fear and Create Trust

Formal incentives and PA&R methods obviously control behavior in organizations. As well as the formal systems, however, informal factors and controls also affect motivation and performance. As W. Edwards Deming and others have recently stressed, informal forces created by the organizational culture can have important effects on incentives and the motivation to perform. As with the more formal forces affecting behavior, these effects of the company climate can have either positive or negative results. One such cultural manifestation is the level of fear felt by managers in a company.

The psychologist Abraham Maslow taught us a long time ago that people cannot strive for greatness or satisfy their higher needs if they're worried about basic physical or security needs. If security is threatened, people hardly can be creative or cooperative. As someone once told me: "Man does not live by bread alone . . . , except when there's no bread."

Because these statements are so obvious, I cringe at the high levels of fear and low levels of trust in many companies. The fear of not meeting all-or-nothing objectives is real. Concerns over the possibility of job loss because of company restructurings, downsizings, or reengineerings are common and debilitating. The fear of performance appraisal and a poor ranking is very prevalent. Fear of telling the truth when it is bad news is commonplace, especially when killing the messenger is the usual outcome. Anxiety about failing and jeopardizing one's unblemished career, lifestyle, pay raise, security, and retirement benefits is quite real.

These fears obviously are counterproductive and destructive to individuals and companies alike. Cooperation on complex tasks that demand shared information and open communication will not materialize or prosper under conditions of fear and distrust.

For cooperation to occur and last, managers must drive out fear and create trust. Clearly, this task is not easy, but I don't think I'm naive in suggesting it. Any step in the right direction is worthwhile, even if fear can never be entirely exorcised from a company. How can management drive out fear and build trust?

Stop Killing Messengers

Killing messengers, as I argued in chapter 6, kills or biases communication. Managers must exercise leadership here. They must create a culture that emphasizes good information and communication. Through example, they must encourage organizational learning, not organizational lying. How does one foster learning?

Consider a situation in which increased product quality is desired. Quality goals are defined, with participation and agreement among key players. Quality is operationalized, processes for improvement are defined, and the information and performance data needed as feedback are agreed upon. The revised work process begins, and feedback about performance is generated. For purposes of discussion, assume that the result is a significant negative deviation between desired and actual outcomes. Quality goals are not met.

For learning to occur, the next step is critical. It is not productive to make excuses or to lay blame. Rather, it is necessary to explain and understand. Managers must facilitate learning, not motivate lying.

Managers can create this atmosphere by clarifying cause and effect and by changing something with the objective of improving the results. Learning directs attention to the worth of information, whether it constitutes good or bad news. Lying biases information and renders it worthless. Learning enhances adaptation, change, and improvement, whereas lying fosters rigidity, avoidance, mediocrity, and even regression. Learning encourages trust and cooperation, while lying only generates fear, resistance to change, and gradual alienation.

Embrace Error

The preceding discussion suggests that to drive out fear and foster cooperation managers must learn to embrace, not avoid error.

Over two decades ago, Donald Michael compared organizations

that avoided error at all costs to organizations that embraced error.[1] In the former, making mistakes was seen as the result of stupidity, carelessness, poor ability, or some personality flaw. So people did nothing risky. They lied or blamed others. They concentrated on being right, a tactic that generates mediocrity. In the error-embracing companies, mistakes were seen as natural and unavoidable. Errors suggested that managers were trying to be creative or innovative. Energies were directed toward learning and improvement, not hiding and avoiding attention. Some additional comparisons of error avoidance and error embracing are shown in table 7.1.

It seems obvious that most people would work more happily and productively under the error-embracing situation. It seems patently obvious, too, that the trust, lack of fear, and openness of this situation are absolutely vital to the creation and prosperity of a We-Force.

Note that nothing in table 7.1 contradicts or negates the positive aspects of the I-Force. Embracing error generates trust, cooperation, and interaction without creating dysfunctional consequences for individuals or the company. In fact, embracing error seems to correlate highly with risk taking, learning, realism, and a lack of fear, all of which support both individual and cooperative needs.

Empower People

Most individuals see empowerment and the autonomy, responsibility, and trust it implies as positive rewards. Empowerment develops motivated managers. Centralized decision making shapes a work force that waits for orders from above or, at best, one in which proactive behavior is extremely rare. Reactive behavior is the norm, which does not bode well for innovation, creativity, or adaptation. Empowerment and the delegation it implies have strong positive effects. These conditions reflect trust and make it possible for managers to try new things without fear of reprisal. Effective empowerment, then, facilitates communication and cooperation.[2]

Practically speaking, who should be empowered and under what conditions or circumstances? Again, the answer comes from good planning, recognition of interdependence, and the assignment of clear responsibilities. A responsibility matrix identifies individuals and groups to whom authority must be delegated to achieve de-

TABLE 7-1

Differences in Organizations That "Avoid" or "Embrace" Error

	Error Avoidance "Organizational Lying"	Error Embracing "Organizational Learning"
Company Situations/Events		
Control Systems	Top-down, repressive or constraining; emphasis on "being right" at all times	Emphasis on self-control; less constraining; emphasis on getting the facts
When a mistake or problem is alleged	Deny the problem or play it down; if cannot deny problem, emphasis on blaming someone else	Admit the error; determine and analyze the causes so as to prevent recurrence
Individual needs being met	Survival; defensibility of actions and position against threats or accusations of others	Higher-level need satisfaction due to growth, learning, and acceptance of challenge
Setting of objectives and performance standards	Top-down, unilateral; little participation or negotiation; "all-or-nothing standards"	Participative process; effective discussion and confrontation of conflict; goals and performance standards are not "all-or-nothing" or simply "black and white"
Attitude toward change	Resistance to change is high	Embraces change as unavoidable, necessary, and beneficial
Interpersonal Orientation	Guarded; low trust; alienation	Open; high levels of trust; emphasis on cooperation and joint efforts

*See Donald N. Michael, *On Learning to Plan—and Planning to Learn* (San Francisco: Jossey-Bass 1973), for a good discussion of embracing error.

sired objectives. Empowerment entails delegation, resource allocation, and the accountability inherent in the planning process and the assignment of roles or responsibilities that result from it.

Because empowerment and its implied trust are inherently motivating for most managers, it is logical and appropriate to charge empowered managers with responsibilities for teamwork and cooperation. Empowerment appeals to the individual side of motivation, in that it implies autonomy, expertise, and other aspects of enlarged jobs. It also can help to create and sustain teamwork if motivated managers are rewarded for joining cooperative efforts and achieving superordinate goals.

To ensure that their companies are reinforcing the desired behaviors and outcomes, managers must emphasize a number of critical steps or actions.

1. *Determine the required level and type of interdependence.* Good planning identifies the need for cooperation by determining the type of interdependence needed to complete the task. When responsibility plotting uncovers overlapping tasks or the need for joint decision making, cooperation is clearly vital to successful performance.

2. *Establish measures of cooperation.* The next critical step is to operationalize useful and valid measures of cooperation. The effects of cooperative effort cannot be tracked, evaluated, or modified if the outcomes of cooperation are not measurable.

3. *Base incentives on cooperative goals.* Incentives must support the right things. For teamwork to be taken seriously, it must be recognized and rewarded.

4. *Revise PA&R methods.* PA&R reinforces certain behaviors and outcomes and reduces the likelihood or others. The single most important step is to reward teams or groups as well as individuals for performance results. Saying cooperative effort is important is not sufficient; it is necessary also to recognize and reward joint effort in formal processes of PA&R.

5. *Create a positive climate for cooperation.* Formal incentives and PA&R methods obviously influence cooperation. What often is not as obvious are the informal forces or aspects of company culture that also vitally affect cooperation.

To ensure or reinforce cooperation, it is imperative to eliminate fear, create trust, and set the right example for subordinates. The informal organization and company culture must support formal methods of recognizing and rewarding cooperation if it is to flourish in a company as a sustainable competitive advantage.

As this chapter has stressed, rewarding desired behavior is critical to increasing it. Appropriate incentives and controls are central to the creation of a We-Force and the cooperation it requires. While this observation may seem obvious, the dysfunctional behaviors noted throughout this chapter are still going on in our companies.

Can we change? Can we learn to concentrate on and reward cooperative efforts that increasingly will be necessary to compete and survive in the future? Or will we continue the foolish, harmful, and counterproductive actions that inhibit the development of a We-Force? The answer, quite frankly, is up to you.

8

Improving Coordination and Cooperation in Geographically Dispersed Organizations

Geographical dispersion—a challenge to cooperation / Effective coordination across large distances / Application of We-Force tenets to a difficult situation

> I really wanted to help [a client company] get a nice loan package for his operations in Brazil. After all, we work a lot of deals for the company worldwide, and banking is getting terribly competitive. But I must admit, I didn't know the person who handles this type of loan there, so I mailed the materials I had to the "Loan Manager" in Brazil. I really don't even know if anyone got the paper or helped the customer.

This comment from a manager in a global bank underscores the problems of communication and cooperation in companies with widespread operations. Geographical dispersion creates management difficulties. Companies with decentralized operations have trouble communicating and cooperating across great distances. "Out of sight, out of mind" is a maxim that rings true in the world of geographically dispersed manufacturing plants, offices, and marketing operations. Cultural differences in international markets only exacerbate problems of communication. Costs of coordination and control are high when interdependent company units are spread all over the globe.

This chapter applies the advice and suggestions of previous chapters to communication and cooperation among company locations separated by large geographical distances.

The problems of coordinating effectively across dispersed operations to achieve the benefits of global competition are well-known and costly facts. But national companies with operations in different cities, states, provinces, districts, or regions face many of the same problems. Global dispersion is the most complicated arena in which to achieve coordination and cooperation, but the advice offered here about dealing with widely scattered operations in Tokyo, Singapore, Chicago, Italy, and San Francisco clearly has application to managers worrying about coordinating operations between New York and Seattle or even Philadelphia and Washington, D.C.

Geographical Dispersion: Realities, Problems, and Solutions

Global competition is here to stay. So are the problems it creates for managing worldwide, dispersed operations. A recent article in the *European Management Journal* identified some typical problems of coordinated global strategies that have implications for a We-Force and effective cooperation.[1] These include the following:

- Coordinating areas of core competence across country boundaries to achieve optimal leverage and create competitive advantage in different parts of the world.
- Overcoming problems of communication caused by different languages, customs, and cultures.
- Training managers to be effective integrators of operations that are far apart.
- Managing and controlling the tensions between units that think globally and others that act locally with a narrower geographical or market focus.
- Developing a core language so that managers anywhere can communicate effectively and quickly.

- Creating organizational structures that mediate conflicts and facilitate coordination and timely decision making across widely dispersed locations.

The bottom line is that global strategies demand complex planning and implementation skills. Some of the same skills, abilities, and techniques apply to all companies that do business across scattered locations. Let's take a look at these skills, and the decisions and techniques that are required to improve coordination and cooperation.

Planning and Recognizing Interdependence

Consistent with the advice in earlier chapters, the first requirement is sound planning. And perhaps the most critical aspect of sound planning is accurately identifying and preparing for interdependence in the geographically dispersed firm.

Assume, first, the relatively simple case of pooled interdependence. Under this form of organization, units or parts of a company are separated geographically, but there is little or no need for active communication, coordination, and cooperation. Integration of the different parts is not needed or, at least, is not common.

Figure 8.1 shows a hypothetical case of such a company. The firm has operations in many parts of the world, but each group or division is autonomous. The division in Brazil makes and sells goods there, while its counterpart in Britain does exactly the same in its markets. Each division focuses on its country or region and has decentralized, autonomous operations. Profit responsibility reflects this separation and independence, as each country or region is an individual profit center.

The divisions work alone together. There is no need to coordinate across country or regional boundaries. The company cannot achieve synergy or competitive advantage by leveraging the production in one country into benefits in another country or part of the world.

Manufacturing laundry soap or chocolate, for example, is focused on geographical areas, with operations selling within the area. No benefits gained within a geographical area—for example, because of lower factor prices, proprietary technology, or labor laws—can be leveraged for competitive advantage in other parts of

Example of Autonomous Geographical Operations

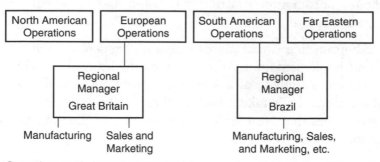

Operations are independent (Pooled Interdependence). There is no/little need for lateral coordination or cooperation.

Figure 8.1

the world. Similarly, brewing and selling beer usually focus on operations within geographical areas. Not only is there nothing to be gained from coordination across sales regions, but high transportation costs limit the viable range of sales activities. Market saturation is achieved by having divisions or operations located in many different geographical areas; each focuses on its market and is not concerned about coordination and cooperation across markets.

The same situation holds if the company in figure 8.1 had units in New York, San Francisco, Miami, and Dallas that cover different sales regions. The regional manager in New York runs a profit center, as does the general manager in San Francisco. Each is independent, and little if any coordination is needed across the separate regions. Interdependence is very low, with each region acting as a little company that focuses on a geographically limited market.

This case is clearly simple and managing this situation is relatively easy. The standard procedures, profitability measures, and company policies governing each geographical unit are basically the same. Overall corporate strategy under pooled interdependence still must ensure that the separate, autonomous pieces are contributing logically and consistently to the whole. Headquarters' evaluations, however, concentrate on individual profit centers, singly, as there is no need to evaluate performance that depends on cooperation or shared operations.

The coordinated global strategy is quite another case, for now interdependence is sequential or complex, to use the terminology developed earlier. Instead of the vertical type of independent organiza-

High Levels of Interdependence Across Geographical Operations

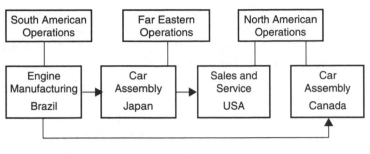

Figure 8.2

tion shown in figure 8.1, this form of competition is better represented by figure 8.2. While the latter figure is still simple, it shows the lateral flows of services, products, or expertise across operating units.

For the company shown in figure 8.2, communication, coordination, and cooperation are important to overall company performance. Quality standards and performance characteristics of engines may vary depending on whether they are used in Japan or Canada. Differentiating and ensuring performance and quality, then, becomes an issue, as does feedback on quality, performance, and customer satisfaction.

Scheduling and planning requirements are clearly greater and more important in figure 8.2 than in figure 8.1. Coordinating flows of product effectively to avoid both excess inventory and stockouts is critical, especially given the distances the products must travel. Just-in-time delivery systems are obviously more difficult to manage and coordinate as geographical distance increases. Given the nature of interdependence in this situation, what steps can be taken to ensure or facilitate communication, coordination, and cooperation among the dispersed operations?

Structures and Processes for Communication and Coordination

A number of ways to achieve effective communication and coordination when company operations are dispersed are explained in the following sections.

Use Informal Methods

The simplest and most common technique is informal contact. A manager in New York or Detroit calls or sends a fax to a counterpart in Tokyo, Mexico City, Sao Paulo, or San Francisco. Delivery dates or scheduling problems are discussed and ironed out. Feedback on product performance, maintenance issues, or other aspects of user satisfaction is analyzed.

The national service department in the United States may call engine quality control in Brazil (see figure 8.2) to discuss a spate of oil leakage or consumption problems in a popular four-cylinder engine. Preliminary discussions take place about potential causes of these engine shortcomings, and an agreement is reached on the next steps in analyzing and solving the problem. Each manager undertakes to create a local ad-hoc team to examine the data available on the correlates or conditions surrounding the problems. A deadline is set for action, with an agreement on when and how the teams will share and analyze their data and findings on the problems.

Informal, direct contact between or among managers is arguably the most common form of everyday communication and coordination. Yet even this simple tactic cannot work without same basic underlying prerequisites for success.

First, *know whom to contact.*Knowing the people, positions, and responsibilities in other locations is vital to cooperation. A directory of key personnel in different geographical locations and their responsibilities is the first essential ingredient in successful informal communication and coordination.

Second, *go direct, not through channels.*People who can solve problems without getting approvals galore or going through their bosses, their bosses' bosses, and so on to contact people directly in other offices or parts of the world usually can make informal contact work effectively as a communication and coordination technique. In contrast, the delay or modification of requests as they pass through channels or undergo numerous checks and approvals often destroys or detracts from the speed and spontaneity of informal, personal contacts.

Managers, then, must review their companies' policies on checks, balances, and permissions. Excess bureaucracy must be eliminated and people must be given direct access to other parts of the organization. Without managers knowing it, over time company policies and procedures can build and grow into bureaucratic obstacles that inhibit the flow of vital information and communication.

The final prerequisite for successfully using informal methods is *understanding roles and responsibilities.* Knowing when direct contact is necessary and authorized, when decisions can be made by lower levels without hierarchical approvals, and whom must be consulted before a decision or informed after one is a function of role negotiation and clarification. Managers must know not only their own responsibilities and authority but also those of others involved in a decision or action. Without clarification of duties, boundaries of decision making, and ultimate accountability, decisions will be avoided. Even simple lateral communication and cooperation will not work effectively.

If managers feel that important decisions are falling into the cracks, role clarification and negotiation using the responsibility matrix discussed previously are clearly in order. This process will help identify accountability shortfalls and job overload, both of which impede communication across dispersed company operations. Analysis may reveal, for example, that no one is accountable formally for coordination across company units. Having identified this obstacle, jobs can be changed and agreement reached as to who is responsible for this critical task.

Even simple, informal methods of achieving communication across different regions of geographically dispersed operations will not work if the three preceding prerequisites are not met. As basic as these steps may sound, collectively they help ensure the everyday interaction and information exchange needed for effective cooperation.

Have a Common Language

To achieve effective communication and cooperation, it is vital that all managers in the company speak the same language. Common language refers to consistent definition and use of important terms like investments, profits, and engineering terminology. The same language must be used across dispersed units of the company.

As odd as this may seem, people in the same organization often are not on the same page when communicating on important matters. They bring different perspectives, technical capabilities, definitions of key terms, or cultural biases that detract from their ability to see and understand divergent points of view. Selective perceptions caused by functional myopia, regional differences, or limited views of problems and opportunities get in the way of shared ideas and common understanding. To develop and sustain a common language, a number of points or requirements deserve management's attention.

Define common objectives and measurements. Misunderstanding begins and cooperation ends when individuals see different outcomes as important or define goals in divergent ways.

Return on investment or return on sales mean quite different things to a division manager pushing one line of products worldwide and a country manager responsible for all the products in his geographical zone. For the former manager, carrying lots of inventory is a requisite for sales of her product. To the latter manager, inventory costs like bank financing are part of the profit calculation that the division manager doesn't deal with or care about. The division manager focuses on her sales and margins only; the country manager must examine sales and returns from many products to find the optimal balance in his product portfolio. If the division's products are not very important to that mix, the two managers' ideas of optimum returns, net profits, and effective market performance will vary markedly.

Common objectives, then, must be defined. Measures of performance must be consistent and agreed upon. Measuring revenues in gross terms, in one case, and sales minus inventory carrying charges and interest expense, in the other, will keep both managers constantly at odds on what constitutes good performance.

Define terms and use the same language. In global competition, language differences are common and problematic. A core language that all key managers can speak is vital to communication. English has become the most common core language among the largest global players, and its use helps to facilitate communication, avoid idiomatic differences in terms, and eliminate changes in meaning in the translation process. However, this trend does not absolve English-speaking managers from learning as much as possible about the language, business customs, and culture of the countries with which they are working. Successful cooperation often depends on commonalities, besides language, that facilitate communication and working together.

Common computer systems and uniform information and control procedures help create a common language and understanding. An aerospace company with different computer systems in each operating division can hardly share consistent views and definitions of critical project milestones or measures of value added in the production process. Use of common systems, terms, and technical language overcomes most of these problems and forces managers to focus on the same data and performance measures across divisions.

Create a common vision. A credo or statement of corporate vision can help to create common goals and approaches to problem solving. A credo's definition of key corporate priorities, stakeholders, and what constitutes the right behavior for all people in the company, regardless of product division, function, level, or geographical location can facilitate communication and understanding across company units.

Managers must analyze their company's languages—spoken, technical, computer—to ensure that common usage and understanding are the rule, not the exception. Cooperation between individuals, groups, or divisions is hampered when information systems, key measures of performance, and other data or languages are not widely understood, compatible, and commonly agreed upon.

Use Teams and Task Forces

Structures and processes to aid effective communication and coordination across dispersed company locations include teams or task forces. These can be either:

- Ad-hoc, or informal, set up for a particular reason and then dismissed upon completion of a task.
- Formal, permanent structural units responsible for ongoing analysis or problem solving across geographically separated units.

In the example shown in figure 8.2, a quality assurance group may be responsible for ongoing analysis of engine performance as well as improvements in engine technology. A team in Canada may evaluate engine performance and submit recommendations for change in design or assembly to the Brazilian manufacturing facility. Or a group representing engine design, manufacturing, and service requirements in Japan and Canada can meet to change engine specifications to reduce service problems. Regardless of the type of team or task force, certain conditions discussed in the chapters above must be met.

Clear goals. The purpose of the team must be clear and understood by all dealing with it. The benefits expected from the team should be stipulated as specifically as possible. The logic and underlying contribution of cooperation must be clear.

Appropriate composition. The make-up of the team must reflect the problems or opportunities at hand. Composing a team for the wrong reason (e.g., politics or a power play to block a country's action) is usually obvious and the team is seen as illegitimate, silly, or dysfunctional. Membership must reflect the requirements of the task at hand, such as a team of engineering, manufacturing, and service representatives to solve the engine problems.

Clear responsibilities and accountability. Precisely what the team can do, to whom it reports, and within what time period—that is, its duties and accountabilities—must be clarified. Is the team merely an advisory body, or can it make and implement decisions? If it makes decisions, how will its actions and results be gauged? The role clarification techniques and responsibility matrix discussed previously work for teams as well as for individuals.

Sufficient resources. Teams that must work across geographically dispersed operations need resources commensurate with their tasks. To extend the preceding example, a task force to redesign the four-cylinder engine with the leakage and oil consumption problems may include Brazilian engineers and manufacturing and service representatives from Japan, Canada, and the United States. To complete their task they may need travel budgets and advanced telecommunications and computer-linking capabilities. Setting robust goals for cooperative endeavors and then not providing the requisite support can only result in failure.

Appropriate and logical incentives. An earlier chapter admonished managers to reward cooperation and lateral communication, and that lesson holds here, too. In a global company, for example, providing incentives to learn foreign languages beyond the core language can help create global managers and add flexibility to a system of rotating job assignments. Similarly, linking promotion or raises to membership and performance on a team that solves cross-regional problems would motivate effective team performance. Understanding, measuring, and rewarding the contribution a group makes to the company will increase the members' feelings of self-worth and accomplishment, as well as gaining them external recognition and appreciation. If global task forces are seen as stars, there is more incentive for participation than if the they are viewed as groups of "dogs" or expendable managers.

Teams or task forces can be effective vehicles for lateral communication and coordination in the geographically dispersed enterprise. If the critical conditions for success hold, a team will perform well and will not be seen as one more useless committee.

Establish Matrix Organizations

One of the most common and best-known structures for achieving coordination in geographically decentralized organizations is the matrix organization. Matrix forms are used to coordinate, communicate, and resolve conflicts around a dual, simultaneous focus. Put another way, a matrix system ensures that coordination and cooperation occur among units with different goals, performance measures, or operating focuses.[2] Consider the hypothetical company in figure 8.3. The company has many independent product divisions worldwide. Each is geographically organized. Each division sells its own products and is a profit center, and the interdependence among divisions is low. The view of the division manager is global; she must worry about selling as much as possible around the world to maximize revenues and profits.

The company also has an international division that is organized geographically by region and country. Each country manager is responsible for sales and profits within his own country. Products and services often need to be adapted to a particular country's culture, needs, or tastes. Hence, the country managers' perspective is decidedly more local. Not all the company's products may be suited to a country manager's market. Rather, the local managers will want to pick and choose from among the various divisions' offerings to optimize the product mix within their countries.

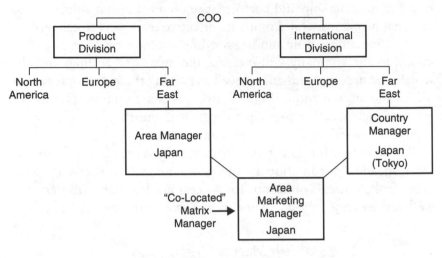

Figure 8.3

In this situation, the global view of the product division and the local view of the country managers must be melded and made consistent. Products, advertising, distribution, and service must reflect local conditions, including consumer tastes, government regulations, and cultural idiosyncrasies. But products, advertising, and distribution must also reflect the need for scale economies and coordination across countries to ensure an integrated and consistent global strategy.

These design requirements demand communication, coordination, and cooperation between division and country managers. Differences in goals and perspectives (global versus local, worldwide homogeneous product versus locally adapted product) can lead to conflicts or disagreements. Geographical separation of key divisional and country decision makers can exacerbate or stall conflict resolution and injure communication and cooperation.

Who should facilitate this interaction, communication, and coordination? The area marketing manager, who reports to both the country manager and the divisional area manager for the same country (Japan in figure 8.3), is responsible. He or she is "co-located," a two-boss manager reporting formally to two different people in charge of Japan. The product or division manager may be located in Japan, at divisional headquarters, or in the Far Eastern regional office. Whatever the situation, the co-located area marketing manager must work across geographical boundaries to link divisional and country needs.

Area marketing managers must facilitate lateral communication, coordination, and cooperation between a division and country. They also must negotiate changes in broad product and service requirements for adaptation to local needs and tastes. Managers in this position must confront, mediate, and solve the conflicts that arise naturally from divergent global and local views.

The matrix structure is complex, despite the apparent simplicity of figure 8.3. Multiply the divisions and the area marketing managers representing them in each country and you have a structure pushing many products. At the same time, country managers are trying to delimit, change, and adapt products to local conditions. Political and power considerations are also part of the equation. Who breaks ties or has the final word on a product—the division or country manager? When all of these factors are considered along with the array of two-boss managers, the violations of unity of command principles, and the tendencies toward disagreement and conflict, the complexities of such a structure become eminently clear.

The matrix relies on effective two-boss managers, but dual control is difficult for some individuals. Similarly, the task of coordinating divergent, conflicting views is more problematical for some co-located managers than others. Global managers are made, not born, and the job of making effective matrix coordinators is not easy.[3] Still, the matrix can be successful in companies with wide geographical dispersion, where the focus must be simultaneously on global and local concerns, and where ongoing lateral coordination between geographical regions and product-line personnel is routine. The matrix structure provides a forum to confront issues and adapt products and services worldwide. It allows for management and coordination of diverse operations across geographically separated sales regions or countries.

Similarly, the matrix structure works for geographically separated units within a country. A division building a complex product (e.g., a satellite) may require coordination across units or functions with divergent performance goals—for example, performance versus cost. The matrix form can help integrate the units, mediate conflicts over different performance requirements, and generally facilitate communication around common goals (e.g., serving a government customer).

What have prior chapters suggested to make a complex matrix structure work effectively? A number of suggestions have merit.

Proper training and planning. The logic of the matrix must be clear to all involved. Planning must generate agreement on the need for and contribution of this structural form. Determining interdependence—where the dual focus exists—and how co-location will handle it must be understood, especially by the two-boss managers.

Simply put, effective communication and cooperation cannot occur if individuals don't understand the need and purpose for a matrix. Involving the affected people in planning or training sessions at the initiation of matrix methods is vital to success.

Agreed-upon tie-breakers. When the co-located integrator cannot resolve conflicts between dominant groups in the matrix (division and country managers in figure 8.3), a mediator or tie-breaker is essential. Someone must have this role. Use of role negotiation techniques and responsibility plotting, as discussed in chapter 5, is suggested.

If a tie-breaker is not identified and charged with this responsibility, decisions can get lost in the process of going up two hierarchies (product division and geographical organizations in figure 8.3). Consequently, the matrix will be faulted for bureaucracy and ineffective handling of disputes. Sound planning and agreement on where the tie-breaking responsibility lies is vital to the success of this structure.

Effective performance appraisal. Who evaluates the two-boss manager? The two bosses, preferably. If only one does so, the two bosses are not equal and the co-located manager will be motivated to serve the more influential side of the matrix better than the other. Incentives and controls, including performance appraisals, formal feedback, and rewards, must reflect the realities of the matrix. Inconsistencies will work against cooperation and communication.

The use of informal methods, common language, teams, and formal structures can facilitate communication and cooperation across geographical distances. When effective planning has identified interdependence or the need to cooperate, and the desired outcomes of cooperation have been defined in measurable terms, these informal and formal methods can facilitate communication and integration around common or superordinate goals.

Effective Incentives

When interdependence has been recognized and structures and processes to manage interdependence and the coordination and communication it demands have been set up, care must be taken to ensure that the whole system really works. One critical need, consistent with advice in earlier chapters, is to ensure that incentives motivate the desired behavior. Appropriate incentives must fuel and support cooperation within the context of interdependence and coordination already set up. The task presently is to discuss how incentives affect and control cooperative behavior in the geographically dispersed firm.

The first point to emphasize is that geographical separation in itself can discourage the desire to communicate and actively coordinate job requirements. When cooperation is seen as difficult, it will be avoided if incentives don't reinforce the cooperation. Even worse, if cooperative efforts are seen as taking too much valuable time and hurting individual rewards and recognition, these joint efforts will be avoided like the plague.

Consider the following, fairly common situation. A corporation wants a particular core competence to be shared across geographically dispersed SBUs to achieve synergies and related benefits from the common skills, resources, or expertise. The corporate view is lateral and seeks to motivate cooperation among corporate and SBU staff and among SBU managers who must work together to facilitate sharing.

SBU heads, however, see the sharing and requisite lateral communication and coordination as taking inordinate amounts of time and effort. As profit center managers, the SBU heads are more apt to focus on the profitability of their own units. In their view, time and effort expended on SBU performance is much more likely to lead to reward than the same effort spent on sharing and working together. If they believe that cooperation will detract from individual bonuses and recognition, joint efforts become even more improbable.

The situation is characterized by different views, values, and motivations at the corporate and SBU levels (see table 8.1). Different incentives are operating for the corporate and SBU staff. The desired cooperation and sharing of core competence will not occur if the corporation does not provide appropriate incentives.

What can be done to motivate cooperation in this situation? Applying the concepts developed previously, corporate management can take steps to motivate and facilitate the desired communication and coordination across the dispersed SBUs.

Define measurable corporate goals. If cooperation had already occurred and the desired synergy across SBUs had been realized, what differences would result? What performance measures or outcomes for the entire company would be directly affected? Desired outcomes here might include economies of scale or scope, improved overall company profit, stock price appreciation, or a clear technical advantage resulting in new corporate patents. Whatever the targeted outcomes, they must be stipulated and measurable.

Reward SBU contributions to company performance. If SBU efforts at lateral coordination and communication positively affect corporate goals, such efforts should be included in formal performance appraisals. SBU managers should receive bonuses or positive appraisals based upon company profits, stock price appreciation, or patents won—not just SBU profitability. Being rewarded for company-level performance will motivate the cross-SBU efforts that lead to improvement of the whole corporation.

Fund certain SBU efforts from corporate budgets. Assume that increased travel is required for SBU managers to integrate programs and activities across the geographically dispersed units. If travel expenses detract from SBU profitability or compete with other uses for the scarce funds, SBU managers will not be motivated to pursue lateral coordination and cooperative efforts. If the corporate level covered all SBU expenses relevant to cross-site integration and communication, the probability of the desired cooperation would improve dramatically.

The realities of organizational life include scarce resources and a desire to maximize the return on them. If cooperation across dispersed company units is seen as wasting resources or offering little return on one's time and effort, the motivation to engage in joint

TABLE 8-1
Corporate Versus SBU Levels

Corporate	SBU
"Big picture," company view	More limited SBU focus
Company performance	SBU performance
Stock price appreciation	Increase in SBU power
Sharing laterally, across SBU's	Working vertically, within the SBU
Coordinating across geographically dispersed units	Avoiding the time and effort required to work across geographical distances

Differences in motivations
and incentives

cooperative projects will be extremely low or nonexistent. Only when the results of cooperative efforts are noted, measured, and rewarded will those efforts become commonplace occurrences in companies.

Effective Control and Information Systems

Control systems provide feedback. They provide information about actual performance versus the level of desired performance suggested by objectives, budgets, and so on. Controls and information are important to change and to the ability to learn from past successes and failures. Organizational learning and evolution are impossible without the feedback provided by effective control and management information systems (MIS), where effectiveness is defined in terms of useful market surveillance, industry analysis, and the tracking of company and competitor performance.

One important aspect of effective MIS was discussed previously in this chapter: sharing a common language in an organization. Emphasis here is on consistent measures of performance and the information that sends signals to managers about individual, unit, or company performance. A common language results in uniformity, consistency, and applicability of the feedback to all managers sharing the same MIS or control system. Despite geographical dispersion, then, individuals in similar jobs or situations must have access to relevant data about their own and their peer groups' performance within the company.

The need for common information and language also emphasizes the importance of valid information. Organizations are rife with data. Only a small subset of the data, however, may be useful and applicable to managers in different locations. A common language facilitates getting the right information to managers, even though they are in different geographical areas.

When MIS is effective, feedback is appropriate, useful, and valid. Country managers in Sao Paulo, Mexico City, and Miami can share and learn from feedback on their own and their peers' performance, regardless of differences in currency, interest rates, and trends in inflation across regions.

One additional aspect of MIS is vital for the effective management of geographically dispersed units in a company—the timeliness of feedback used to judge cooperative performance. There clearly is a need for speed when communicating and coordinating decisions across large distances.

Refer once again to figure 8.2 and the hypothetical team set up to analyze and solve performance problems in a four-cylinder engine. The team comprises individuals from different functions (manufacturing, assembly, sales and service) and countries (Brazil, Japan, the United States, and Canada). Functional biases may be present, and certainly one might expect cultural or regional preferences on critical variables like engine cost and performance. Similarly, functional or geographical differences may exist in desired warranty requirements and the useful life of the engine, both of which affect costs and the rate of engine replacement.

Assume that the team has agreed to experiment with a variation in engine design calculated to increase torque, acceleration, and other aspects of performance while, simultaneously, controlling warranty and service expense. Team members decide on the experimental engine design and the performance information needed to test their hypotheses and assumptions. They set up a model, choose the factors or conditions to alter, and then return to their respective units and geographical areas to await the results.

For communication, coordination, and cooperation to work,

timely information is critical. Speedy or frequent feedback is required to reinforce team goals and the importance of team membership. Without timely information about key engine parameters and performance, interest among geographically dispersed members will wane. Without frequent and useful reminders of the team's job and importance, conflicting job pressures and other more immediate tasks will ensure that out of sight means out of mind. Local issues and pressures without frequent feedback and contact will spell disaster for global coordination and cooperation.

To ensure effective management across geographical distances, then, MIS procedures should emphasize a few critical points in the name of timeliness.

Stress common information. Managers from different job functions and locations must be on the same page of the plan. Measures of performance and cost must be relevant, useful, and valid, regardless of geographical and functional differences. Cooperation across dispersed units is improbable if people perceive gross differences or inequities in the key variables used to gauge performance or test the experimental model.

Reengineer information Technology. Modern computers and information technology make it easy to capture and disseminate vital data over vast distances. MIS systems enable the geographically dispersed company to distribute knowledge, coordinate inputs, and facilitate decision making. Powerful computers allow the organization to treat decentralized operations as if they were centralized. Most importantly, the capturing and sharing of relevant data can be accomplished quickly, ensuring that decision making and coordination can proceed in a timely and efficient manner. To ensure effective management, then, the geographically dispersed company should invest in modern information technology and use it to facilitate rapid communication across vast distances.

Emphasize timely feedback. Quick and repeated feedback gives a sense of urgency and centrality to the issue being addressed. It calls for action. Such feedback may even help create a sense of excitement, especially if feedback suggests some success in the team endeavor. Timely and frequent feedback from MIS provides an excuse for team members to communicate, travel, and worry about their joint task, despite geographical separation.

These aspects of MIS or control systems—a common language

coupled with timely or frequent feedback—are often overlooked in the large, geographically dispersed company. Even though the need to standardize communication and to motivate individuals to communicate across distances is obvious, it is seldom emphasized. Without the commonality of information and purpose and the motivation to discuss common goals, cooperation cannot be sustained.

This discussion has focused on ways to improve communication, coordination, and cooperation across geographical boundaries, a common and difficult situation facing many companies. A number of key steps are necessary to achieve effective performance in the geographically dispersed organization.

Plan for cooperation. The first step is sound planning, including agreement on the nature and difficulty of coordination and communication among separated units. Determining the degree or type of interdependence is key here, as complex forms of interdependence will tax coordination and communication networks. Pooled interdependence provides few problems, but the flow of materials or services indicated by sequential or reciprocal interdependence necessitates more elaborate methods of lateral contact across geographically separated units.

Focus on coordination. When interdependence is high—that is, when geographically separated units must communicate and actively coordinate activities—methods of achieving lateral integration include the use of individuals, teams, and formal matrix-type structures. The easiest form of lateral coordination is direct, informal contact. Use of teams is more difficult, while formal matrix organizations are the most complex of the structures designed for coordination and cooperation among dispersed company units.

Eliminate barriers to cooperation. Common obstacles to interaction and communication include bureaucratic hurdles, such as going through channels, getting permissions to communicate across different functions or company units, and justifying the travel and other expenses required to coordinate activities across great distances. Unnecessary bureaucratic barriers to cooperation must be identified and eliminated or work across dispersed units will be seen as a troublesome burden and assiduously avoided.

Clarify responsibility and accountability. Use of the responsibility matrix is critical to defining jobs and responsibilities in the geographically dispersed firm. Potential problems include no clear accountability for communication, coordination, and cooperation across interdependent company units. Without such responsibility and accountability, the motivation to make things happen across multiple units will be low or nonexistent.

Measure the results of cooperation. It is a waste of time and effort to talk about cooperation but develop no measures or outcomes to represent it. The results of communication, coordination, and cooperation across company locations must be operationalized and developed into clear, measurable objectives. The outcomes of cooperative enterprise must be tangible, measurable, and important. Otherwise, cooperation sounds good but means nothing. Feedback using the measures reinforces performance and signals the value of cooperative efforts.

Provide incentives and rewards for cooperative results. Managers will make the effort to achieve integration across geographically distant units if they are rewarded for doing so. Focusing on measurable results and forging a link between cooperative outcomes and rewards will motivate managers to tackle the difficult task of coordinating and communicating across geographical distances. Without this positive feedback, the needed efforts will not materialize.

Working with different locations need not be a daunting problem or managerial dilemma. Lateral communication, coordination, and cooperation are possible and worthwhile endeavors. All that is needed is a bit of effort to focus upon the requisite conditions outlined in this chapter. The outcomes and results achieved will be worth the time and attention.

9

Making Joint Ventures Work

*Why joint ventures? / Difficulties in
making joint ventures work / Ensuring
success of cooperative ventures*

Our experience with joint ventures [JVs] has been disappointing. Some companies are very slow to act as JV partners; their headquarters must check and approve everything. Others are looking for quick profits. They want our technologies and ideas immediately, but often hold back on bringing their skills to the table. Some companies even try to hit and run—make a profit or gain some advantage and then desert the venture completely. We've decided that long-term competitive advantage doesn't come from JVs, but from investment in our own company.

Joint ventures and other forms of strategic alliance are extremely popular. They represent a form of cooperation between two companies that can be lucrative and mutually advantageous. Yet as the preceding statement from a Japanese manager suggests, making JVs work can be quite difficult, even frustrating.

Of all the forms of cooperation, joint ventures are probably the most difficult. All of the typical barriers to cooperation are multiplied when two or more companies agree to a strategic alliance. Cooperation is made even more difficult by the fact that the partners may continue to compete in areas outside of their venture.

This chapter explains the conditions that make JVs successful. As in the last chapter, the key issues for cooperation are integrated and emphasized while answering the pragmatic question of what makes JVs work.

Joint Ventures as Cooperative Efforts

JVs and related forms of strategic alliance are logical and practical solutions to increasingly common business problems. These problems (and opportunities) emanate from ever-changing competitive and technological conditions as well as from the inability of traditional forms of organization to keep up with the rapid pace of change. The factors that make JVs attractive include competitive, technological, or administrative conditions that only recently have become pervasive concerns of management.

Rapid Technological and Market Change

One critical underlying reason for the proliferation of JVs and other strategic alliances is the ever-escalating rate of technological change. Firms facing this situation find it difficult to remain on the leading edge technically. Developing its own technological skills and prowess is an increasingly costly and risky business for a company. Heavy R&D investment can be negated quickly by a company's leap-frogging competitors. Rapid technological change creates many options, but if one company's product becomes the industry standard, then the others lose out—a very costly loss.

In a related vein, rapid changes in markets, distribution channels, or consumer preferences can create problems for a firm. If changes in customer needs or distribution requirements (e.g., speed to market, need for new products, rapid change in product specifications) are accompanied by technological upheaval and the necessity for different production processes, the firm faces a tough task in keeping up with the rapidly changing situation.

One solution is not to try to keep up in isolation, but to join with others who are keeping up or surpassing the firm in technology or in meeting the market. Joining forces in a JV allows a company to tap knowledge, a new technology, or a distribution channel in domestic or foreign markets quickly. Each firm need not reinvent the wheel repeatedly but can bring its expertise to the bargaining table in exchange for another company's knowledge, skills, or resources.

The recent JVs in the pharmaceutical, information, computer, electronics, and automotive industries are based on the desire to share scarce resources, avoid duplication of effort, and gain access to new markets.

The Shortcomings of Organizational Structure

A related reason for the rise of JVs derives from the shortcomings of previously popular organizational designs. Structures that worked and led to competitive advantage in the past are being severely challenged by the rapidity of technological and market changes.

Consider just one example, that of vertical integration (VI) backward or upstream. VI as a strategy works best and optimizes costs under certain conditions, all of which strengthen a company's competitive position. These conditions include the following.

High demand for a company's products, with low sales volatility. VI produces the best results when a company has predictable, steady, high-volume demand for its product or component. Volatility and low demand wreak havoc with production schedules. They also force downtime or production stoppages in the VI unit, thus forcing the parent company to carry a heavy burden of fixed overhead expenses and high variable costs per unit of output.

Little technological change. Investing in upstream technologies is more logical when the technologies are relatively stable. Upheavals in technology can render a major investment virtually obsolete. Lack of up-to-date technology in the VI unit can put the parent company at a competitive disadvantage. Investing in VI under conditions of high technological change or volatility is very risky, at best.

Control over a proprietary technology. If upstream VI leads to competitive advantage through the control of a vital skill or proprietary technology, such a move makes sense. If the strategy offers no proprietary position because numerous other companies supply similar or the same inputs, it doesn't make sense.

A high degree of VI places a company in a position of disadvantage when the preceding three conditions are not met. Similarly, highly structured bureaucracies or oppressive hierarchies in companies can slow response time to customers and markets. The need for speed in relation to changing market conditions demands more nimble, quickly adapting organizational forms.

The logic of JVs under conditions of rapid market and techno-logical change, then, is derived from the firm's ability to gain com-petence or expertise without developing it itself. JVs allow a com-pany to stay up to date without the burden of high investments and technological risks. Such alliances increase a company's ability to adapt and achieve speed to market because needed technologies and distribution channels need not be developed in a costly, slow, or cumbersome manner. This form of cooperation presents a clear win-win situation for the parties working together and sharing their skills, knowledge, or technologies.

Problems in Making JVs Work

Despite the obvious benefits of cooperation, JVs often don't work. Despite the logic of sharing scarce resources and avoiding risky in-vestments that can be rendered obsolete under volatile market and technological conditions, partners in the cooperative ventures often abandon the joint arrangement. What are some of the reasons for this apparently illogical behavior?

Conflicts between short- and long-term perspectives. Suppose that one partner in a JV develops a skill because it is looking for a long-term competitive advantage. The other, in contrast, has a short-term view and wants to borrow and use the skill for quick ad-vantage. The borrowing company desires a fast benefit, but has lit-tle to offer the partner with the longer-term view. Conflicts develop and produce distrust and holding back by the player with the long-term view.

A shotgun approach. Some companies enter many JVs in the hope that some will work. This scattering of efforts prevents the companies from paying adequate attention to any of the coopera-tive ventures. As a result, the JVs dissolve.

Unclear or suspect goals. The shotgun approach and even less scattered attempts to establish JVs encounter problems because the goals of the partners are unclear or suspect. Each side is suspicious of the other's real motives. Each sees the other as trying to gain and run, so that the partners distrust each other and hold back. The JV partners perceive disingenuous, calculative motives in each other, not the candor, logic, and desire to share evenly that must mark the cooperative relationship.

A win-lose mentality. JVs depend upon reciprocity and sharing of scarce resources so that each side perceives a win-win or synergistic situation. Lack of a perceived bilateral benefit or feelings of distrust can lead one partner to feel exploited. It develops a win-lose mentality that is detrimental to the cooperative arrangement.

Invalid or incomplete information. The success of a JV relies in large part on each side knowing its own strengths and the competencies of the potential partner. Poor competitor analysis or inadequate market surveillance can lead to incorrect assumptions about what a partner brings to the table. Of course, the JV is terminated as soon as the party with preconceived notions learns the truth about another company's shortcomings or competencies.

The problems outlined in the preceding paragraphs and similar obstacles can deliver a formidable challenge, if not a fatal blow, to the potential venture. What can be done to avoid problems and make the JV a viable and profitable form of cooperation? Again, earlier chapters provide some clues on how to make JVs work and prosper as cooperative arrangements.

Making JVs Work
Building Cooperation

Companies desiring JV partners often presume that the logic or mutual benefits of cooperation are obvious. Consequently, they spend little time or effort on activities to solidify the bases of joint effort and make them work. However, making JVs work entails a number of important analyses and purposeful actions, without which the shared venture is on shaky footing.

The firm seeking a lasting strategic alliance must plan carefully. Instead of a scattered shotgun approach to JVs, the metaphor should be a few well-chosen and well-aimed rifle shots. The latter model suggests carefully analyzing what a JV can accomplish and then actively seeking a partner to create a mutually beneficial form of cooperation.

Careful planning for strategic alliances involves four critical steps:

1. Accurately noting and understanding your company's strengths and weaknesses.
2. Examining industry and competitive forces to determine the factors or resources critical to success in the industry.
3. Matching your company's strengths and weaknesses against the critical factors required for industry success.
4. Compensating for critical weaknesses through establishing purposeful and carefully chosen JVs.

Let's consider each of these four steps separately, showing the logical interdependence among them. Without this type of analysis, those hoping to set up JVs may focus on acquiring the wrong skills by contracting with inappropriate partners.

Accurately assessing strengths and weaknesses. This step seems obvious, but it can be problematical because of company inertia, functional myopia, or political sensitivities. These problems notwithstanding, the first critical planning-related step in making JVs work is an accurate self-analysis of a company's particular skills and shortcomings.

This analysis can be facilitated by modifying the nominal-group technique described in the appendix of chapter 4. This technique focuses on (a) generating a viable list of issues, like problems, opportunities, or strengths and weaknesses; (b) discussing items on the list in ways that maximize participant involvement and visible agreement; and (c) developing a priority ranking or importance rating for the items that can guide future decisions and actions.

Identifying critical success factors in the industry. The next step is to perform a careful analysis of industry forces and major competitors. While traditional industry analysis identifies a broad array of forces and variables that affects competition and profitability in a market, the analysis suggested here is more focused. Specifically, the purpose of this analysis is to identify the industry conditions or company resources that are critical to success. The task is to determine what resources, skills, or control over industry forces will boost a firm. The analysis can focus on the entire industry or segments of it, depending on the strategy and focus on the company.

The results of the first two steps in the planning process can be

**Company Strengths and Weaknesses, and Industry Success Factors:
Matching Revenues for Success**

Company Skills/Capabilities	Critical Resources for Success	Less Important or "Neutral" Resources
	A	**C**
Major Strengths or Competencies	• Low cost producer • Plant location • Distribution channels	• Custom engineering skill • Government relations
	B	**D**
Weaknesses or Shortcomings	• Full product line • Service capability • R&D specific technological skills	• Long term contracts with suppliers • Modern office facilities

Figure 9.1

combined and positioned for analysis in a matrix like the one in figure 9.1. This figure depicts the basis of the third step in the planning process for JVs.

Matching company strengths and weaknesses with factors needed for industry success. In figure 9.1, the critical quadrants are A&B. Company strengths are valuable if they contribute to success in the industry or chosen market segment (quadrant A). Company strengths, in contrast, mean little if they contribute little or nothing to performance in the market place (quadrant C). Company weaknesses are dangerous and competitively disadvantageous only if the firm is weak in areas that are vital to success in the industry or a chosen market niche (quadrant B).

The importance of the matching exercise outlined in figure 9.1 is to understand that strengths and weaknesses, in themselves, mean little. They become significant only when they are compared and analyzed within the framework of industry or competitive requirements for success.

Identifying JV partners. Quadrants A&B are central to aligning with a JV partner. In essence, quadrant A shows what qualities or company strengths may be attractive to a potential JV partner. Quadrant B identifies critical areas where the company's weaknesses can cause major operating or strategic problems. The company must attack the shortcomings noted in quadrant B, because avoidance can only lead to poor performance or competitive disadvantage.

One way to attack the critical weaknesses noted in quadrant B is via JVs and similar cooperative alliances. The company can trade its skills or competencies for the strengths of another company that can fill the void suggested by Quadrant B. The JV might exchange access to one company's massive, productive channels of distribution for the other's R&D or technological capabilities.

Sound planning, then, is the critical first step in making JVs work. Careless shotgun approaches are not productive. The company must identify exactly (a) what it brings to the bargaining table to attract JV candidates, and (b) where it is dangerously weak before industry and competitive forces and, thus, where the help of a cooperative alliance is needed.

The competitor analysis performed as part of the planning stage can help identify the firms that have the skills and capabilities to help the company make up for its competitive weaknesses. Without these aspects of sound planning, a JV clearly begins its life on shaky footing.

Stipulating Areas of Interdependence, Goals, and Incentives

The form of interdependence under JVs is usually reciprocal, as discussed in chapter 5. Reciprocal interdependence connotes a mutual dependence in which each firm gives something and gets something in return. Each company is dependent on the other, so each is simultaneously strong and vulnerable to some degree in the exchange relationship.

The perceived dependence and vulnerabilities can generate problems early in the JV process. Fears and a reluctance to show one's hand or skills can lead to immediate threats to cooperation. What's needed for the JV to work is a contract stipulating each firm's responsibilities in the cooperative venture and other vital operating conditions.

Defining the conditions governing shared resources. The extent to which companies share each other's strengths or capabilities must be stipulated. How distribution channels are to be jointly used, for example, and whose products receive preferential treatment under what conditions must be agreed upon.

Generating agreement. Agreement on goals and how to achieve them in the JV, including how to share skills and expertise, is vital to the specification of mutual dependence and responsibilities. The assets of the JV are the resources of each firm and agreement on their use is vital to JV success.

Breaking ties and resolving conflicts. Conflicts are sure to develop over the sharing of resources created by interdependence. Methods to resolve conflicts and break ties must be instituted. An executive committee with managers representing both JV partners, for example, could be charged with the tie-breaking role. In the absence of such techniques, unresolved conflicts can lead to deep-rooted animosities and poor communication between JV partners, thus threatening cooperation and the reciprocal nature of the venture.

Partners in the cooperative ventures also must share their goals and the conditions that motivated them to pursue the JV. In the absence of such clarification, each side may ascribe a hidden agenda and devious motivations to the other. This suspicion can lead to distrust, a reluctance to communicate openly, and, ultimately, a failure of cooperation.

Keep in mind that partners in the JV may be competitors in certain markets. The cooperative agreement usually does not cover all resources, technologies, or parts of the world. A fierce competitive arena may still exist outside of the areas covered by the JV.

This competitive reality reinforces the need for partners to clarify goals and motivations in the cooperative agreement. The specter of competition can easily overshadow the benefits of cooperation. It can lead a company to attribute destructive goals and motives to a JV partner.

It is far better to openly document the goals and forces motivating participation in the common venture. Each side must see that both sides are driven, in part, by selfish motives. If each side understands the incentives for the JV and knows where they compete with and support each other's desired outcomes, the trust, openness, and perceptions of mutual benefit suggested by the JV can flower.

No JV is perfect. The incentives and ambitions of the parties rarely dovetail or overlap precisely or uniformly. Each side, after all, is seeking competitive advantage in areas where it is weak. This incentive is logical and should be part of the formal stipulation of the JV goals, conditions, and outcomes.

Setting Up Structures and Processes

Establishing formal structures to facilitate communication, coordination, and control within a JV is very tricky. The JV in many respects represents a quest for simplicity in organizational arrangements. The model is reminiscent of an age-old system of barter and mutual exchange. Parties to the JV usually seek an informal relationship and seem to eschew the formal and rigid forms of hierarchical structure that typify the large bureaucracy. The JV represents a desire to pursue a simple professional relationship based on agreed norms and benefits to both parties in the cooperative relationships.

Unfortunately, despite the quest for simplicity and informality, the JV needs formal structure to survive. It needs some control to ensure coordination, communication, and achievement of the outcomes for which it was created. Information exchange and openness are vital to the cooperative venture. They are also needed to ensure trust and mutual respect, as lack of communication can engender distrust and fears that a JV partner is following a hidden agenda and pursuing unilateral benefits.

The antagonism between the need for formal structures and the desire for the informal, simple arrangement envisioned by JV participants must be confronted by the management of partner companies. Prescriptions in previous chapters have emphasized the need to facilitate communication and coordination under conditions of reciprocal interdependence. The same logic must be applied to the JV, although those designing the procedures must be careful to avoid creating a stifling bureaucratic system of rules, hierarchies, and excessive documentation of rights and responsibilities.

I have emphasized the need for a contract between JV partners that stipulates each side's responsibilities and privileges. This contract should focus on: the goals of the JV and the outcomes anticipated by the partners, the conditions that govern the development of shared resources, the incentives and benefits that motivated the formation of the cooperative venture, and processes for resolving conflicts between JV partners.

This contract should be complete, yet as simple as possible. Trying to anticipate every problem, exigency, or potential area of disagreement and building procedures up front to deal with them can only lead to excessive documentation, stifling formality, and legal nightmares. It is far better to construct a simple agreement and then rely on other structures and processes to facilitate communication and handle nonroutine matters as they occur—for example, the executive committee mentioned previously. If the documentation is too formal, it breeds rules, a search for loopholes, and an early resignation to the fact that the JV is encumbering, not helping, both parties.

What actions can be taken to ensure sufficient structure and process to foster communication while avoiding the stifling documentation and bureaucracy of formal legal structures? A number of steps can foster communication, coordination, and control, assuming the existence of the JV contract.

Designate managers responsible for JV operations. Each partner in the cooperative venture should designate a manager with overall responsibility for making the JV work. These managers are at once integrators and informal liaisons who remain in touch and provide direct, informal contact between JV partners. Similar to managers of change during restructurings or mergers, they are dedicated to the venture and represent a visible sign that the JV is sufficiently important to pay specific attention to it.

Use cross-organizational teams. These teams can be ad-hoc and informal, or they can be set up as permanent bodies. Their purpose can vary by JV, but generally their role is to: (a) foster communication between partners, in addition to interactions of the responsible managers; (b) handle ad-hoc problems that arise in normal JV operations and resolve conflicts; (c) regularly evaluate the JV's performance against agreed-upon goals and other contract conditions; and (d) provide feedback to JV partners on performance or recommended changes in shared operations.

Develop management information systems to facilitate feedback and review. Partners in strategic alliances usually have separate MIS capabilities that handle their own information and control needs. However, JVs may demand a customized, dedicated MIS system. If partners rely only on their individual, uncoordinated systems, they risk breeding selective perception and disparate evaluations of JV performance. It is necessary to:

• Develop timely and valid information about JV performance. A dedicated MIS capability must measure performance and other outcomes that are relevant to the JV and then speedily provide information that is useful for decision making.

- Monitor JV performance and provide feedback to cooperating partners. Feedback is vital to the continuation of the joint effort. Continued surveillance and feedback help to ensure that the JV has the requisite flexibility to adapt and change over time, thereby continuing to provide incentives to JV partners to sustain their cooperative behavior.

The steps outlined in the preceding paragraphs help to ensure effective communication and coordination between or among JV members. JVs are characterized by high interdependence and, by definition, the need to cooperate to achieve common goals. By using individuals and teams to coordinate activities and by developing MIS capabilities to monitor JV performance, the partners can feel confident that the cooperative venture is achieving the desired results and will remain an effective vehicle and motivating force for the parties involved.

JVs and other strategic alliances are cooperative arrangements whose performance and sustainability are affected by a number of aspects of the We-Force thinking covered in this book. These include:

- Showing the logic and mutual benefits of the JV. This step presumes that the results of cooperative effort are measurable, important, and mutually satisfying to JV partners.
- Overcoming the common obstacles to cooperation, including poor communication and distrust between partners that result from inadequate planning, ineffective MIS capabilities, and lack of agreement on JV goals.
- Ensuring that the incentives to sustain the JV and keep it as a viable, productive alliance remain positive over time. Individuals and companies who may be competitors in some arenas certainly need positive incentives and continued reinforcement to cooperate in others.

The JV, then, is nothing magical or unique. Like other cooperative forms, ventures, or systems, it requires the attention of management to survive and thrive.

10

Conclusion

Can managers pull off the changes recommended in the preceding chapters? A better question is: "Why haven't we changed already?" Much of what I've argued or addressed has been experienced by many savvy managers. Indeed, individuals were probably adding their own war stories as they read.

If the war stories are so plentiful, even pitiful, why do so many companies still engage in mistakes and foolishness that are so commonly recognized? Why are so many still repeating mistakes? Is change possible? Let's explore these issues.

Why Haven't Companies Changed?

If cooperation and a We-Force are desirable, why are we still fostering "win-lose" competition, killing messengers, creating fear, communicating poorly, and not rewarding teamwork. What accounts for this apparently foolish and inexplicable behavior?

First, old habits die hard. Inertia is a difficult obstacle to overcome. Things change slowly, if at all, even when there's ample reason to do so. The problems are obvious, yet managers keep muddling through, seemingly oblivious to the dangers about them.

Individual self-interest is strong in the United States. The tendency is to keep doing what's known and comfortable, even if conditions have changed.

In addition, intensely individualistic behavior has worked before.

It's been useful, so why not stick with it? Great things aren't accomplished by committee, so why focus on anything other than individual needs, drives, and rewards? The I-Force helped us win a revolution, motivated us to go West, enabled us to expand our frontiers, grow, take what we wanted, be profitable, and so on. Why change things now, why argue with success?

The second impediment to change is that our individualistic habits have been reinforced over time. The I-Force, as well as many of the debilitating behaviors noted in earlier chapters, have been amply rewarded and reinforced. Managers have learned the game and passed it on to successive generations.

We've learned, for example, how to lie and low-ball, while ostensibly doing sound planning. We've learned not to be the bearer of bad tidings, for we know what happens to these messengers. We know how to cover our butts and avoid risk, despite the calls for innovation. We've learned that risk taking is fine—if our choices are right.

Remember, too, that incentives and controls are conceptualized and defined by managers who have learned the rules of the game. Incentives support individual performance and feedback, not teamwork or cooperative effort, because that's the way things have always been. Despite refined incentive plans, individual performance and recognition are somehow all that matter. Getting ahead is still an individual concern. The more some things change, the more they remain the same.

Why Must We Change?

I've said this before, and I'll say it again: the I-Force is useful and desirable, but it must be channeled in new directions. Individual motivations are fine if they result in joint or cooperative effort. Why are cooperation and a We-Force vital and necessary at the present time? What's different now? Why must U.S. mangers change their thinking? I have touched on some of these points before, but they're important enough to emphasize in closing.

The frontiers are changing rapidly. The rapid expansion of the country and growth in GNP that marked earlier portions of this century are gone. The ambition and aggressiveness to go west, take lands, conquer the environment, find gold, and so on aren't needed today to the same degree.

We're at a different point on the growth curve, so to speak. Now that the period of expansive growth and the many opportunities it provides have waned, many U.S. and global markets are facing a more mature, more competitive, and less munificent stage. Under rapid growth, there's enough to go around; individual aggressiveness is fine. With slowed or no growth, winning involves taking things from others, which can occasionally be dysfunctional. As one exec told me:

> We still spend more time, effort, and money competing within the company than with outside competitors. It's one division against another, both for internal resources and, and in some cases, for the same customer outside in the market. What the hell's wrong with us? Don't we have enough competition already from the Japanese, Koreans, and Europeans? Why do we have to fight among ourselves, with people who supposedly are on the same team?

As economic frontiers constrict, competition becomes more intense and potentially more deadly. As the preceding quote indicates, U.S. companies are being buffeted like never before in all markets. And intensity of competition is inversely related to profit margins. More than ever, companies must produce a high-quality product at a low cost to be competitive and survive.

With increased competition, cooperation becomes more necessary. Intense internal competition within U.S. companies that results in win-lose situations and units hurting other units to look good and hoard more resources clearly is dysfunctional and undesirable. Cooperation, sharing, superordinate goals, and the overall good must enter managerial thinking for U.S. companies to survive.

We have to face the fact that the global marketplace is here to stay. This form of competition is no longer the exception but the rule in most industries. Global competition is creating more need for coordination and the best use of scarce resources. Leveraging a comparative advantage in one country into a global competitive advantage demands cooperation and effective coordination, not just knowledge of products or markets.

Global competition also gives rise to a need for other forms of cooperation, such as joint ventures, strategic alliances between companies, and enhanced government–industry partnerships in key industries. Competitive conditions are changing, making cooperation and the conditions that define the We-Force necessary for survival.

We Must Change

We must change our ways of thinking. We must eliminate the barriers to effective communication, coordination, and cooperation that currently exist in our companies. The next decade or so will be brutal and costly if managers continue to muddle through, relying on past practices and hoping that somehow cooperation and effective performance will result.

What will companies have to do to survive and prosper in the 1990s and beyond? The following points summarize needs or issues that are critical to future success.

A need to focus. The business world is getting too complex for companies to be all things to all people. Smart management is learning to create core competencies or distinctive competencies that give it leverage across all markets or products. Consider the following two hypothetical questions: "What percentage of the worldwide market in compressors do we have? What percentage of the refrigerator market do we have?"

The former question draws attention to a core capability (compressor technology), not just a particular product or market segment. The latter question might drive a company to outsource or buy compressors. The former question wouldn't allow such a strategic error, for excellence in compressor technology is what is seen as driving the company's success across all products or markets.

Core competence or distinctive capability is critical to success in tomorrow's complex markets. The task facing management is how to define, measure, create, and sustain a competence or set of skills that is truly at the core of what a company does. Having some capability is one thing; having a distinctive competence that separates a company from its competition and gives it a sustainable advantage is quite another.

A need for speed. Companies must learn to respond better and faster to markets and customers. Competitive advantage more than ever will be difficult to sustain over time. Innovation and new product or service development will become the norm, the ongoing need of business, not something that's done in sporadic, discrete steps. Getting things off the drawing board and into the market in an expeditious and timely manner is one accomplishment that will increasingly differentiate successful companies.

A need for flexibility. The days of the bureaucratic monolith are disappearing. Companies that can be flexible, allowing them to move more quickly than their competitors, will gain advantage in the more fluid, dynamic, and demanding markets of the future.

A revitalized work force. Managers and workers must take responsibility for actions and decisions. At all levels, individuals must be empowered to act. Delegation increasingly will be the norm, not the exception. To achieve speed in innovation, get close to customers, react quickly to competitive pressures, and avoid bureaucratic ills and obstacles, the manager of the future must feel free to act and take risk. Costly and time-consuming approval processes and reliance only on top-down wisdom must give way to an energetic, empowered work force that feels confident enough to make decisions and take action.

Our Needs and Challenges Demand Cooperation

Of course, many different needs and challenges face our companies, but those mentioned here seem to be vitally important and typical of what managers will be forced to worry about in the coming years.

The central point for us presently is that meeting these challenges require a great deal of cooperation. Most of these changes demand better communication, coordination, appropriate incentives, and many of the other critical correlates of cooperation noted in this book.

The development of distinctive competencies, for example, demands cooperation and coordination across organizational units. Divisions or SBUs cannot stand as independent silos, in defiance of technological and other developmental thrusts that cut across products or markets. Sharing rather than hoarding must be the operational norm if synergy and core skills are desired.

Innovation and speed in responding to customer demands are based necessarily on good communication, feedback, and the ability or power to act quickly, without fear of mistakes or reprisal.

A flexible company and a revitalized work force thrive on empowerment and delegated responsibility. Cooperation and adaptability require a basic level of trust and confidence as well as the requisite levels of expertise.

Successful innovation, change, and cooperative efforts demand that these desired outcomes be rewarded and reinforced by the company. Incentive and control systems must generate the right behaviors. They must support change, risk taking, cooperation, recognition of interdependence, superordinate goals, and so on. Otherwise, desired outcomes won't materialize and, increasingly, companies will realize a competitive disadvantage. To summarize, the critical spurs to cooperation include the following steps.

Harness the I-Force

It isn't necessary to negate or thwart individual motivation—but it must be focused on desired superordinate goals. The importance of cooperation and teamwork will increase in direct proportion to the reinforcement these behaviors receive and their perceived importance in relation to individual goals and achievement. We-Force thinking can be consistent with the individual needs and drives, if the tenets discussed in this book are followed.

Focus on Good Planning

Sound planning efforts concentrate on the generation of agreement or consensus as well as on sound strategies and objectives. Planning facilitates participation in decision making, which breeds commitment to cooperative efforts.

Good planning also enables mangers to recognize interdependence, which defines the arena for cooperation. This understanding enables managers to lay out the areas where joint decision making is vital to success and provides the logic and impetus for teamwork.

Facilitate Communication

Saying that communication is vital to success may sound trite and simplistic, but communication is a core requirement for cooperation and teamwork. More than ever, managers must realize that shared problems are already half solved. And sharing demands common language, good data, information-processing capabilities, and other aspects of sound communication.

Managers must identify and eliminate barriers to effective communication. Whether they are structural, power-based, geographically influenced, or the result of poor incentive and control methods, the barriers must be identified. Then they must be supplanted by the methods noted previously to facilitate and motivate the effective sharing of information. Cooperation and teamwork are not possible without good communication.

Reward Teamwork and Cooperation

Above all else, it is critical to recognize and reward teamwork. Mangers cannot hope for cooperation while rewarding different behaviors. Companies cannot espouse cooperation but reward only individual performance. Appraisal methods cannot routinely reinforce win-lose situations, excessive competition, and a "get them before they get you" mentality and still seek cooperative behavior.

Teamwork, cooperation, communication, and other aspects of a We-Force are too important to leave to chance. If desired, they must be operationalized, measured, and rewarded.

Can we change? Can we cooperate better? Can a We-Force flourish simultaneously with an I-Force? Can teamwork coexist and feed upon the intensely individual drives that have been typical of U.S. managers for so long?

I hope so. But, quite frankly, it's up to you, the managers reading these words. If you wait for others to begin doing the right things, nothing will happen. Do something, change something, and others will follow.

Leadership by example is critical here. Regardless of level or function—CEO or middle manager, strategic planner or operations planner, marketing manager or R&D specialist—good managers can find something useful in this book and do something in their own companies. Good managers lead by example, innovate, and teach others that change is possible. The future performance of many companies is vitally linked to the emergence and persistence of these leaders and their intense belief in the value of cooperation and teamwork.

Notes

Chapter 2

1.   Max Weber, trans. T. Parsons, *The Protestant Ethic and the Spirit of Capitalism* (New York: Scribner & Sons, 1958).
2.   David McClelland, *The Achievement Motive* (New York: Appleton-Century-Crofts, 1953); *The Achieving Society* (New York: Van Nostrand Reinhold, 1961).

Chapter 4

1.   For a good discussion of empowerment, delegation, and shared decision making, see: William F. Joyce, *MegaChanges: Reforming the Corporation* (New York: Irwin Professional Press, 1994).
2.   For more on the relationship between strategy and structure, see: Lawrence G. Hrebiniak and William F. Joyce, *Implementing Strategy* (New York: Macmillian, 1984); and Lawrence G. Hrebiniak, "Implementing Global Strategies," *European Management Journal,* Vol. 10, December, 1992, 392-403.
3.   Andre Delberg, Andre Vande Ven, and D. H. Gustafson. *Group Techniques for Program Planning: A Guide to Nominal and Delphi Process.* (Glenview, IL.: Scott, Foresman, 1975).

Chapter 5

1.   James D. Thompson, *Organizations in Action* (New York: McGraw-Hill, 1967).
2.   For more on responsibility plotting, see: Jay Galbraith, *Designing Complex Organizations* (Reading, Mass.: Addison-Wesley, 1973); L. G. Hrebiniak and W. Joyce, *Implementing Strategy* (New York: MacMillan, 1984).

Chapter 6

1.   Remark to the author. See also Russ Ackoff, "Management Misinformation Systems," *Institute of Management Sciences,* vol. 14, no. 4, December 1967.

2.   See W. Edwards Deming, *Out of the Crisis* (Cambridge, Mass.: MIT Center for Advanced Engineering Study, 1989); and William W. Scherkenbach, *The Deming Route to Quality and Productivity* (Washington, D.C.: CEEPRESS Books, 1988).

Chapter 7

1.   For a good discussion of embracing error, see Donald N. Michael, *On Learning to Plan And Planning to Learn* (San Francisco: Jossey-Bass, 1973).

2.   For an excellent discussion of empowerment and related issues, see William F. Joyce, *MegaChanges: Reforming the Corporation* (New York: Irwin Professional Press, 1994).

Chapter 8

1.   Lawrence G. Hrebiniak, "Implementing Global Strategies," *European Management Journal,* Vol. 10, December, 1992, 392-403.

2.   For more information on matrix structure, see Jay Galbraith, Designing Complex Orgaanizations (Reading, Mass.: Addison-Wesley, 1973); Stanley Davis and Paul Lawrence, Matix (Reading, Mass.: Addison-Wesley, 1977); Lawrence G. Hrebiniak and William F. Joyce, *Implementing Strategy* (New York: Macmillian, 1984).

3.   For a good discussion of how global managers are developed and used, see William Taylor, "The Logic of Global Business: An Interview with Percy Bartnevik, *Harvard Business Review,* March-April 1991.

Index